IØ121846

Stina Torjesen and Indra Øverland, Eds.

International Election Observers in Post-Soviet Azerbaijan

Geopolitical Pawns or Agents of Change?

SOVIET AND POST-SOVIET POLITICS AND SOCIETY

ISSN 1614-3515

Recent volumes

Stina Torjesen and Indra Øverland, Eds.

INTERNATIONAL ELECTION OBSERVERS
IN POST-SOVIET AZERBAIJAN

Geopolitical Pawns or Agents of Change?

ibidem-Verlag
Stuttgart

Bibliografische Information der Deutschen Nationalbibliothek
Die Deutsche Nationalbibliothek verzeichnet diese Publikation in der
Deutschen Nationalbibliografie; detaillierte bibliografische Daten sind im
Internet über http://dnb.d-nb.de abrufbar.

Bibliographic information published by the Deutsche Nationalbibliothek
Die Deutsche Nationalbibliothek lists this publication in the Deutsche Nationalbibliografie;
detailed bibliographic data are available in the Internet at http://dnb.d-nb.de.

Note: This is the second publication from the project *Network for Election Observation and Exchange* which focuses on Moldova, the Caucasus and Central Asia. The key aims of the project were to enhance the participation of observers from the region in international observation missions and to facilitate local research on the role of election observation in democratic development.

∞

Gedruckt auf alterungsbeständigem, säurefreien Papier
Printed on acid-free paper

ISSN: 1614-3515

ISBN-10: 3-89821-743-4
ISBN-13: 978-3-89821-743-9

© *ibidem*-Verlag
Stuttgart 2007

Alle Rechte vorbehalten

Printed in Germany

CONTENTS

INTRODUCTION

Stina Torjesen & Indra Øverland

Azerbaijan's parliamentary elections in November 2005 became an arena where domestic and – according to the contributors to this volume – international actors battled for influence and control, using both formal and informal means of contestation. This book highlights the role of international observer missions in the 2005 election processes, and presents in-depth assessments of the pre- and post-election situation in Azerbaijan.

The six articles presented in this volume have been produced by leading scholars and development practitioners in Azerbaijan. This is the second scholarly publication within the project 'Network for Election Observation and Exchange', which focuses on Moldova, the Caucasus and Central Asia. The key aims of the project have been to enhance the participation of observers from the region in international observation missions and to facilitate research on the role of election observation in democratic development. Further information on the project is presented at the end of this introduction.

The 2005 elections in Azerbaijan are interesting for several reasons. First, the conduct of elections sheds light on the level of democratisation in a country. In addition, assessments of oil-rich Azerbaijan offer interesting insight on the relationship between energy wealth and democratisation. Second, the elections in Azerbaijan received considerable international attention. They were seen as a test case of whether the wave of regime change that had affected Georgia, Ukraine and Kyrgyzstan would spread to other countries in the region. International actors, regional and global powers and multilateral organisations, were thought to play important formal and informal roles before and after the elections. Third, the role of Russia in the election process was particularly interesting. For the first time, a large number of Russian observers served within the Office for Democratic Institution and Human Rights

(ODIHR) election observation mission; Russia's distinct involvement in the election process seemed to signal new trends in Russia's strategy towards observation and observation missions in the post-Soviet space. Fourth and finally, the case of Azerbaijan also highlights the methodological and technical aspects of election observation. Among other things, there was extensive – and arguably problematic – use of exit polls. Azerbaijan has also recently introduced a comprehensive election law, which significantly altered the administration and conduct of the elections.

This introduction briefly discusses some of the points mentioned above, indicating key questions and challenges for election observation that arise from a study of Azerbaijan's parliamentary elections. An outline of each of the six articles presented in this volume follows. The introduction ends by offering further information about the 'Network for Election Observation and Exchange'.

A common theme in assessments of the elections in Azerbaijan has been the relevance of international actors to domestic political processes in the country. Multilateral organisations such as the Organisation for Security and Co-operation in Europe (OSCE) and the Council of Europe (CoE) – both of which list Azerbaijan among their member-states – have been particularly prominent. Considerable attention has also been devoted to the activities of key regional and global powers with an interest in the affairs of Azerbaijan, the most significant ones being Iran, Russia, Turkey and the USA. Analytical perspectives premised on geopolitics are often employed in order to make sense of the actions of multilateral organisations and foreign powers towards Azerbaijan. Arguably, however, the case of international rivalry over the election outcome in Azerbaijan highlights both strengths and weaknesses of a geopolitical analytical perspective.

Geopolitics is concerned with the impact on interstate relations of the spatial dispositions of continents and oceans and the distribution of natural and human resources (Agnew, 2003). States with the greatest material capabilities are most likely to survive in the international system. This triggers a competition for resources on a global scale by the most powerful states. Azerbaijan is seen as a country where there is a strong likelihood of strategic rivalry for control and influence by external states – due to its position as an energy producer and energy transmitter, as well its increasingly important military strategic location, i.e. proximity to Iran and to military theatres in the Middle East and Central Asia and its location on Russia's southern border. A key premise of the geopolitical perspective is the assumption that states are unitary and coherent actors that express and implement one unified strategy. Nation states, rather than international organisations or other transnational actors, are given analytical priority.

Assessments of Azerbaijan and the elections that have used geopolitics as the analytical frame have highlighted the competition between Russia, the USA and powers as a central aspect of the 'battle for Azerbaijan' during the 2005 election period. It is certainly true that both the USA and Russia proactively engaged with actors in Azerbaijan before and after the elections. However, there are significant weaknesses in explaining the actions undertaken by these and other actors solely in a geopolitical perspective. Azerbaijan had been a problem for Russia since 1993. The country had refused to be part of Russian-sponsored (hegemonic) multilateral organisations like the Collective Security Treaty Organisation (CSTO), and had used other powers (Turkey and the USA) to counterbalance Russia's influence. In other words, Azerbaijan under presidents Heidar and Ilham Aliev had not been a loyal ally. Russia had been unable to realise many of its strategic interests towards the country, such as control over production and transport of oil and gas. Why, then, should Russia decide to give active and substantial support to Ilham Aliev's factions in the parliamentary elections of 2005? Why not support factions that could guarantee better future terms for Russian interests? Why back a political leadership with proven past and present links with what is generally regarded as a key adversary of Russia in the region – the USA?

Geopolitical assessments do not provide adequate answers to these questions. Moreover, geopolitical frameworks tend to underplay the role of actors from within the country when accounting for why events unfold as they do. There is little tangible evidence available, which could prove that the USA or Russia played roles beyond being important advisors, facilitators and endorsers of various political actors in Azerbaijan, including the opposition and the political leadership. The central players in the events during the elections were the local and central levels of government as well as the various factions of the opposition movement and other political parties. A geopolitical perspective, however, diverts attention and explanatory focus away from local

dynamics and the formal and informal strategies employed by domestic actors – and as such may be ill-suited to further our understanding of Azerbaijani politics.

A geopolitical assessment would not expect US and Russian interests to
coincide in Azerbaijan in the way they did – both offered support (in the form
of overall recognition of the election result) to Ilham Aliev and the political factions loyal to him. In contrast, an assessment of regime type offers greater insights into the specific international constellations associated with the election
process in Azerbaijan. Arguably, the key driving force in the international
game for Azerbaijan (as well as other areas of post-Soviet space) is not primarily geo-strategic competition. Rather, the 'fault lines' of the international
relations of the region run, between, on the one hand, conservative local
powers and outside forces that stress continuity and status quo in governing
techniques and leadership, and on the other hand local powers, local forces
and outside powers that seek reform in governing techniques and renewal in
leadership.[1] The first group includes Russia and many CIS countries; the latter includes Ukraine, Georgia, Kyrgyzstan (only partly) and the countries of
Europe and North America. This, arguably, has been one of the central dynamics of the international relations of the region over the past two years.
Such an analytical approach can explain why Russia chose to back previously disloyal segments of the political elite. The importance of regime similarities seems to have trumped strategic concerns.

An additional problematic feature of a geopolitical perspective on international relations of the region is the tendency to overlook the extent to which
the OSCE itself as an institution has become a battleground for the frictions
between status quo and reformist states in the region. The political manoeu-
vring that has taken place within this organisation is, however, a key event in
the international relations of the post soviet area – which deserves greater attention and assessment.

Increasing scrutiny of the work OSCE came with a joint Russia–Belarus
proposal for OSCE reform at the year-end conference in Sofia 6–7 December

---

1   Jennifer Welsh (1999) argues for attention to differing regime dynamics in how inter-
     national relations are assessed. She discusses the international dynamics of revolu-
     tionary versus status-quo states in the context of English approaches to the French
     Revolution in 1789.

2004. Russia raised the spectre of blocking the adoption of the 2005 budget if moves towards reform were not endorsed. Since then, Russia has developed plans to enhance the security co-operation of the organisation and limit the OSCE's work in the sphere of democracy promotion – including election observation.[2]

The problematic role of the OSCE for a country like Russia that supports "status quo" regimes was highlighted during the overthrow of President Askar Akaev in Kyrgyzstan after the parliamentary elections in February and March 2005. Immediately after these events, Russian Foreign Minister Sergey Lavrov stressed that those who tried to destabilise the situation in Kyrgyzstan had used the OSCE's monitoring assessments; he added: 'they [those trying to destabilise Kyrgyzstan] have appealed to these assessments of the OSCE. Russia cannot but note that such a thing was allowed'.[3]

The Russian reform drive in relation to the OSCE has in some ways created greater participation in election monitoring by Russia. Russia and other CIS states have increased substantially the number of CIS observers that serve in CIS-organised observation missions. Russia has also advocated for including a greater share of Russian speakers in ODIHR missions. For the ODIHR election observation mission in Azerbaijan Russia deployed an unprecedented 81 short-term observers (out of 617 short-term observers). However, the Russian observers expressed immediate disagreement with the overall ODIHR assessment. One month later, Russian Foreign Minister Lavrov drew the following conclusions from the Azerbaijani experience:

There definitely are double standards in OSCE's activities, especially in the human rights sphere. This is a fact that cannot be avoided. The OSCE Office for Democratic Institutions and Human Rights proves that with its work on observing elections. At the beginning of November Russia sent a large group of its observers to join the ODIHR mission at the Azerbaijan parliamentary elections. Our observers saw that the ODIHR's work was non-transparent, closed and basically completely alienated from the joint OSCE leadership bodies and from the individual member states as well. This results in biased political opinions made in the OSCE's name although they are not co-ordinated

---

2   Eurasia Daily Monitor, 1 (148), 16 December 2004, 'OSCE "reform" – or a new lease on life?'
3   Itar-Tass news agency, 30 March 2005, 'Kyrgyzstan Trouble-makers used OSCE'; article made available through Lexis-Nexis.

with all member states. Such ways of OSCE's work have to change as soon as possible.[4]

Russia's behaviour and statements raises the question of what its reform drive will imply for the organisation. Will there be a strengthening and prioritisation of the security dimension of the OSCE's work over its activities in the sphere of democracy promotion and election observation? Are these efforts initiated so as to weaken the OSCE prior to the Russian presidential elections in 2008 and to lessen the significance of the OSCE during elections elsewhere in the region? What significance will this have for international election observation missions, including ODIHR?

These new developments also raise direct challenges for ODIHR and other international observation missions. Are there ways in which international observation missions can protect themselves from being caught up in rivalries between reformist and status quo oriented powers in the region? Can further consolidation and awareness on 'objective methodologies' as well as more diverse composition of observation teams strengthen the role and status of observation missions? What should be the relationship between CIS observer missions and ODIHR missions? Are there synergies between the two, with a potential for developing co-operation? Is the increasing attention, and challenge, towards the activities of some observer groups an indication that the international norms of election observation and adherence to democratic procedures may in fact have become more consolidated – more effective, but also more controversial?

These are questions urgently in need of debate – but unfortunately a detailed examination lies beyond the scope of the present volume. Here in this brief introduction the aim is merely to highlight the ongoing challenges facing election observation, and to encourage further research on these issues.

Several of the contributions in this volume touch on some of the questions raised above. The contributions provide for great diversity of views, and it should be noted that the editors do not share all the views of the contributors

---

4   *Financial Times Information*, 7 December 2005, 'OSCE needs reforms, Russia's Lavrov says for Slovene daily', BBC Monitoring, from Lexis-Nexis.

to this volume, but that we do nonetheless believe that they deserve attention.

Leila Alieva in her article 'International observation missions: assessments of the 2005 parliamentary elections' argues that there is a connection between some of the conclusions of the international observer missions and the strategies of some countries have towards Azerbaijan. She outlines the various observation missions and highlights the divergent nature of the reports issued by these missions. Alieva also presents findings related to the conduct of exit polls, and raises serious concern over their use and effect. Her article also discusses the extent to which foreign powers can influence the government and opposition groups in Azerbaijan, and draws attention to the special geopolitical context of Azerbaijan.

In Ulvi Amirbekov's article the focus shifts from international observation to the domestic institutional structures for election observation. 'Frameworks for election observation in Azerbaijan: institutional improvements but little impact?' assesses key past and present features of Azerbaijan's election legislations and describes the evolution of election observation in Azerbaijan since 1991. Amirbekov argues that election observation has become increasingly important in Azerbaijan, but that it nevertheless faces several serious constraints.

Zafar Guliev in his article 'Parliamentary elections in Azerbaijan: democratic expectations versus imitated realities'. He provides a comprehensive outline of the elections held in Azerbaijan since 1995 and compares the recent parliamentary elections to past ones. Guliev identifies key patterns in the strategies of the political leadership during the 2005 elections, and assesses the activities of other domestic and international political actors. He argues that the elections failed to meet important democratic standards and that many features of the elections were poor imitations of a democratic process rather than a real one. Using a geopolitical framework, he assesses the activities of international actors with the use of a geopolitical framework, arguing that Moscow and Washington had common interests in supporting Heidar and Ilham Aliev.

In 'The 2005 parliamentary elections as a mirror of politics and society in Azerbaijan', Zardusht Alizade identifies the key actors of the election process and shows how these players interacted. Alizade argues that the political process associated with the election period highlights core structural features of Azerbaijani society, and, with reference to these, offers explanations for central developments in the political life of the country.

Rustam Seyidov complements Alizade's work with a detailed account of various segments in the ruling elite in 'The post-election situation: who rules Azerbaijan?' Seyidov assesses the behaviour of the leadership during the elections and debates the significance of the role of the opposition politician Rasul Guliev. He also analyses the wave of arrests of top government officials that came just prior to the elections, and offers insights on the political affiliations of certain criminal elements in the country. He concludes with reflections on the present and possible future role of Islam in the politics of Azerbaijan.

In their article 'Economic implications of the parliamentary elections: symbiosis of politics and economics', Torgrul Juvarly and Ali Abasov present insights on how the economic condition of Azerbaijan impacts on politics and governing institutions. Despite frequent reference to oil and its political effects, few studies have examined this central issue in detail.   Juvarly and Abasov present original material that sheds new light on the political life of Azerbaijan. They contend that there is a symbiosis between politics and economy in Azerbaijan, and highlight the interaction between the private sector and the state-controlled part of the economy. They also assess the degree to which institutions designed to regulate the economy operate in a sound manner. As long as the symbiosis of politics and the economy continues, they argue, it will be difficult to ensure a healthy development of Azerbaijan's economy.

Network for election observation and exchange

The present volume is the second publication produced within the project 'Network for Election Observation and Exchange'. This initiative is funded by the Norwegian Ministry of Foreign Affairs and implemented jointly by the Norwegian Helsinki Committee and the Norwegian Institute of International Affairs. It has both a research and a practical component. The research part seeks to facilitate research on election observation and democratic developments in Moldova, the Caucasus and Central Asia. A key aim is to enable and facilitate research by scholars from the region.

Increasingly, international election observers are playing a prominent role in political developments in the former Soviet states. Some election observation missions have been criticised for being too heavily influenced by Western ideas and for unjustly propagating Western standards and practices on these newly independent countries. A core idea behind the project is that election observation should not create a top–down relationship between Western and non-Western countries, but that all countries should have the chance to participate in the international community and be involved in ongoing efforts to strengthen democratic and human rights norms. It was against this backdrop that the Norwegian Helsinki Committee in the first phase of the project invited 24 participants to observe the parliamentary elections in Norway on 12 September 2005. This mission wanted to stress that election observation is not meant solely to reflect power discrepancies between rich and poor countries: it concerns universal standards applicable to all countries, and for which all countries should agree to be put under outside scrutiny.

The project has aimed to facilitate participation in international election observation missions by observers from Moldova, the Caucasus and Central Asia; to strengthen capacity and networking in Moldova, Central Asia and the Caucasus on election observation; and to facilitate research and analysis on the role of election observation in Moldova, Central Asia and the Caucasus for democratic developments in the region.

Key project outcomes from the first phase include:

- 27 observers from Moldova, the Caucasus and Central Asia monitored the Norwegian parliamentary elections on 12 September 2005. A report detailing their findings and suggesting improvements has been submitted by the Norwegian Helsinki Committee to the Norwegian Ministry of Local Government and Regional Development.

- 24 observers from Moldova, the Caucasus and Central Asia monitored the local elections in Kyrgyzstan on 18 December 2005. Their report, with findings and suggestions for improvements, has been submitted to the Central Committee for Elections and Referenda.

• Networking between election experts, researchers and civil society enhanced in the sphere of election observation in the region.

• A web page with election observation resources and news has been launched, http://www.cac-elections.net

• Two publications comprising nine articles by scholars from the region are being produced – one of which is the present volume. The other report offers in-depth analyses of the role of international election observation missions in Kyrgyzstan in 2005

• A seminar has been conducted at the OSCE Academy Bishkek: 'Role, Effect and Status of Election Observation in Central Asia and the Caucasus'.

The first phase is now completed, but the Norwegian Institute of International Affairs will continue to include analytical attention to analytical issues associated with election observation in the period ahead – including facilitating research and publishing relevant analysis.

I INTERNATIONAL OBSERVATION MISSIONS: ASSESSMENTS OF THE 2005 PARLIAMENTARY ELECTIONS

Leila Alieva

1. Introduction

This article argues that the conclusions drawn by international observation missions in Azerbaijan were closely intertwined with the overall approaches and policies that outside powers had maintained with the country. It highlights the divergent nature of the reports and conclusions presented by the various election observation missions. It also discusses the complexity that the conduct of exit polls added to the assessments.

Signals from foreign powers have mattered greatly to the choices made by the government and opposition groups in Azerbaijan. In the case of the USA and Europe, however, their multiple agendas and diverse interests, along with their fear of losing out in security and energy dialogues with Azerbaijan, served to limit their levers of influence on Azerbaijan's government, and the way it organised the parliamentary elections in 2005.

Azerbaijan and the West: Historical Relations

Azerbaijani society had high expectations for the Western (US and European) assessment of the parliamentary elections. The West is perceived as consisting of democratic states: these are expected to promote, and stand for, democratic changes and values in states currently in transition, such as Azerbaijan.

These expectations are also connected with the identity of Azerbaijan. The country made Western integration a strategic priority of its foreign policy, and has joined the Council of Europe (CoE) and the Organisation for Security and Co-operation in Europe (OSCE) as well as developing its relations with the European Union. This trend stems from a deep historical tradition, particularly marked since the second half of the 19th century, whereby the Azerbaijani upper class, elite and intellectuals were leading a reform process aimed at a Western European model. The process manifested itself in the formation of the national industrial bourgeoisie, the development of a multi-party system, the latinisation of the alphabet, the creation of a type of European-style secular education, and other measures. This took place from the 19th to the early 20th centuries, before the occupation by the Bolsheviks.

High expectations among the people of Azerbaijan regarding the West's principled position were also reinforced by the recent shift in the security paradigm of the US administration. The Bush administration had made democracy promotion a priority and an important part of its official rhetoric, and had also supported the revolutionary changes in Georgia, Ukraine and Kyrgyzstan. All these factors created widespread hopes that the West, unlike other external actors such as Russia, would introduce a value-based approach to the assessment of elections, and that this would be an important element of the democracy-building process. The 'value-based approach' (or the 'principled approach') is the opposite of an interest-based approach.

Azerbaijan and the West: Changing Expectations, Growing Apathy

These expectations, however, gradually waned with each election, declining in particular after the 2003 presidential elections. The societal dynamics, on the one hand, and the interests of the external actors, on the other, were often divergent: this was demonstrated in both the 2003 and 2005 elections. While the 2003 elections were characterised by a high level of electoral activism and hope for change, as reflected in the unprecedented high turnout (71.23%), the Western states now seemed to prefer a situation involving a transfer of power to the heir of the president. For this reason – and with the exception of the Embassy of Norway – they gave a very soft assessment of the fraudulent election and post-election violence. This significantly affected the general political apathy of the population and caused a steep drop in turnout – only 46% in the 2005 parliamentary election.

The apathy was also connected with the consistent failure of 'elections' as an institution. According to local observers, the opposition party Musavat had led the race in the 2000 parliamentary elections; similarly, by many accounts, the 2003 elections indicated that the Musavat party leader, Isa Gambar, received a high percentage of the vote. Furthermore, on the eve of the 2005 parliamentary elections, some polls (for instance, the NED-sponsored poll, conducted by the ADAM Centre) showed that the opposition bloc Azadlyg was rated first. All three of the elections were significantly falsified in order to tilt the outcome in favour of the ruling elite.

As to the continuation of the status quo in political developments in Azerbaijan, the interests of all the major external actors (including Russia and the USA) coincided. This was exemplified by the relatively soft assessment of the presidential elections in 2003 made by international organisations, except for the group of 188 observers of the IDEE, and local observers. In some cases there was even direct political support for the 'dynastic' transfer of power.

This left the opposition and civil society isolated in their efforts to change the trend of consolidating non-democratic rule. Most importantly, it limited the chances of building a publicly controlled, democratic institution before the major inflow of oil revenues begins (expected to start next year). Thus, the most recent set of presidential elections in Azerbaijan demonstrated how diverse agendas have affected the conclusions of the external actors in regard to the elections, and how this in turn influenced the future of state-building in the country.

2. Major External Actors

There were three major external actors during the 2005 parliamentary elections in Azerbaijan: the USA, Europe and Russia.

International Delegations

Five delegations from European and Euro-Atlantic organisations were joined in the International Observation Mission:

- OSCE/ Office for Democratic Institutions and Human Rights (ODIHR), which had 43 election experts and long-term observers from 18 participating states, and nearly 500 short-term observers during the Election Day, with Geert Heinrich Ahrens as head of mission;
- the OSCE Parliamentary Assembly (OSCE PA), led by Alcee L. Hastings, President of the OSCE PA and a special co-ordinator for the short-term observers;
- NATO Parliamentary Assembly (NATO PA), headed by Mark Clapham;
- the Parliamentary Assembly of the Council of Europe (PACE), led by Leo Platvoet
- the European Parliament (EP), headed by Marie Anne Isler Beguin – a total of 617 from 42 countries.

The USA and Russia

Although the US assessment was conveyed within the common statement of the International Observation Mission, during the pre-election period the USA continued as an independent and influential actor in the post-election developments in Azerbaijan.

Similarly, although there was a group of Russian observers within the OSCE mission, Russia also sent observers as part of the Commonwealth of Independent States (CIS) and Russian Parliament Missions. Thus, there were three missions with considerable Russian participation: those of the CIS and OSCE, along with the mission of the Russian Parliament itself.

The Larger International Community

As compared to the elections in 2000 and 2003, the 2005 elections in Azerbaijan were characterised by considerable interest on the part of the international community. Besides the observers, the elections were attended by a large group of journalists from some of the world's leading TV channels, newspapers and journals. In total, there were 1,586 foreign observers, 301 journalists and 17,014 local observers.

The whole election year demonstrated a high level of interest on the part of the USA, Europe and Russia – three critical actors in these elections. Their interaction with the Azerbaijani political and civil actors during the pre-election period, both in public and behind closed doors, had the effect, perceived by many, of empowering certain political groups - with particular effect on government-opposition relations. This acted to shape an image of the West, as well as its interests, and not least its policy priorities, in the whole of Azerbaijani society. The year 2005 was marked by several visits by high-ranking members of the US government, the US Congress, European organisations, as well as visits of leaders of the Azerbaijani opposition to the European states and the USA.

Reactions to the External Interest

Government
According to some sources, the Azerbaijani government made extensive use of help from political technologists from Russia, as well as forming a few lobbying groups in Washington DC. They worked intensely with foreign experts, politicians and influential actors. The main objective in the promotion of the government's 'cause' during the international electoral PR campaign was to create an image of the President as a reformer, struggling against a group of conservatives in the government, and facing the resistance of local-level executives. This aimed to prove that there was a strong political will to conduct

free and fair elections, but obstructed by resistance from 'below'. 'Proof' of this political will of the authorities was shown by two presidential decrees (in May and June 2005), directed at improving election practices.

Local People

For the locals, this system had been all too familiar since Soviet times. To them, there could be no doubt that resistance to the improvement of election practices was to be found at the highest level of power. This expressed itself in the resistance of the authorities to agree to the more substantial recommendations of the Venice Commission of the CoE – especially when it came to changing the composition of the electoral commissions, and introducing an inking procedure, which would weaken central control over the election process.

However, local institutions, candidates, and newspapers kept informing the public and foreign observers that there were 'worrying reports' of certain groups ensuring the victory of specific candidates, in continuation of the old tradition of Aliev's communist rule. These groups were reported to include the heads of the district election commissions (who were instructed by the presidential administration), the heads of the executive administration, and policemen and prosecutors of the regions and provinces. Compared to the ruling party, the opposition had very scarce resources at its disposal for international and national PR campaigns. Furthermore, it had limited access to the most influential media channels, such as television, as these channels had been monopolised by the regime ever since early 2000.

Preliminary Conclusions

Compared to the conclusions of the 2003 presidential elections, the preliminary conclusions of the international observation missions during the 2005 elections were tougher. The press conference held by the International Observation Mission on 7 November began with its main conclusion, read by the head of the OSCE mission (a congressman from Florida, Alcee Hastings). His statement was met by applause although Hastings' opening message cautiously described the scale of the violations. State Department spokesman Adam Ereli backed the conclusions of the International Observation Mission on the same day. However, Ereli failed to give a clear answer to the question posed at the press conference as to whether fraudulent elections would have any effect on US–Azerbaijan bilateral relations.

Even though over 80 of the OSCE observers were Russian, the OSCE report strongly condemned the conduct of the elections as falling short of international standards. By contrast, the CIS and Russian missions praised the elections as 'democratic'.

3. International Assessment of Elections

The USA

Mixed Messages

The US position in the 2005 parliamentary elections in Azerbaijan was perceived as inconsistent. While numerous visits and statements of US representatives to Azerbaijan in 2005 signalled a high level of interest on the part of the US government in the upcoming elections, there were also signals that Washington was not in favour of a Ukrainian or Georgian scenario occurring in Azerbaijan. It was (and is still) clear that the situation in Azerbaijan was complicated by the security agenda (anti-terrorist co-operation) and the country's hydrocarbon resources. This might have affected the US support for democracy in this particular case. These circumstances conditioned the ambiguous and mixed-character signals that the USA sent to Azerbaijani authorities and opposition.

On the one hand, it was encouraging opposition through statements which asserted that the Bush administration was supporting democracy all over the world. During the visits of both influential civil actors and congressmen, there were meetings with leaders of the opposition. The strongest message was found in G.W. Bush's inaugural address. In that speech, he set out a radical departure from US foreign policy, stressing solidarity with oppressed peoples everywhere: 'There is no justice without freedom, and there can be no human rights without human liberty.' During a visit to Azerbaijan, Madeleine Albright, former US Secretary of State and head of the US National Democratic Institute, met with leaders of the opposition parties, as well as members of the Azadlyg bloc. Ali Kerimli, leader of the Popular Front Party, said that the two-hour-long meeting with Ms Albright was not only important and useful, but it would also serve as an impetus for the development of democracy in Azerbaijan (Turan news agency, 12 July 2005).

On the other hand, the USA praised the commitment and co-operation demonstrated by the Azerbaijani leadership at the bilateral level. Madeleine Albright stressed that the reasons for the growing interest in the country were its important location, its rich resources, its two big neighbours, its prolonged conflict, and the forthcoming election. In addition to this, she also expressed the hope, belief and expectation that the Azerbaijani people would make a transition to democracy through a peaceful evolution. It is noteworthy that, during his visit to Baku, George Soros concluded that he did not see the grounds for a revolution in Azerbaijan. At a meeting with US Under-Secretary Paula Dobriansky, the Azerbaijani president, Ilham Aliev, focused on the strategic partnership between the two countries. He assured her that Azerbaijan supported the US policy in the area of security and energy. Ms Dobriansky in turn expressed the hope that the Presidential decree the on elections would be fully implemented and that, '(the) US-funded exit polls, conducted by independent, objective organisation', would help to deter election fraud. At a meeting with the opposition, she said that the goal of her visit was to stress the importance that Washington attached to free, fair and democratic parliamentary elections in Azerbaijan, and to deliver the message that she had arrived in Azerbaijan to support the democratic process in the republic. In a statement similar to that of Ms Albright, however, the Under-Secretary stressed that the USA desired that the democratic changes in Azerbaijan should occur through evolution, rather than revolution *(Zerkalo,* 1 September 2005, p. 2).

Similarly, at the end of their August visit to Baku, two US Senators, Richard Lugar and Barak Obama, praised the Azerbaijani president's policy by stating that the report of the electoral administration (concerning election preparations) had made 'a good impression' on them. Lugar made a reference to the opposition leaders, who confirmed that the procedure of registering candidates for parliament passed, 'at a good level.' This he called a 'step forward' compared to previous elections. At a meeting with the president, Lugar made it clear that the practice of repeated voting had to be eliminated, and that the Electoral Code had to be improved and properly applied. He also referred to the issue of a 'velvet revolution' in Azerbaijan. Although his image is connected with revolutions, Lugar stressed that he did not expect a revolution in Azerbaijan. He also thanked Ilham Aliev for the support that the high level of the relationship between the two countries had created, and praised Azerbaijan for its involvement in international anti-terrorism coalitions and for providing an air corridor to enable the conduct of anti-terrorism operations.

The US Congress Resolution

Besides the visits of the US delegations to Azerbaijan, the House of Representatives of the US Congress adopted a resolution (20 July 2005, passed in late October 2005 and additionally passed by the Senate), calling on the Azerbaijani government to hold fair parliamentary elections. Stressing the importance of avoiding any forms of violence (by all sides) during the pre-election campaign, on Election Day, and in the post-elections period, the resolution called on the Azerbaijani authorities to guarantee the freedoms of expression and assembly. This was an unprecedented resolution by the US Congress in relation to Azerbaijan, and indicated the high level of importance that the USA attached to the then-upcoming elections there.

At the same time, by distributing the responsibility for the possible violence between both parties, it softened the warning message to the government regarding the application of force during public protests. Nevertheless, the United States expressed its concerns about state violence in connection with the arrival of Rasul Guliev, and the related events. The statement of the US representative to the OSCE, Julie Finley, distributed on 20 October, noted: 'we remain troubled by reports of police violence during the unauthorised demonstrations in Baku on 9 October, as well as by reports that the police have detained up to 300 political activists, including up to 20 candidates, on 16 October, in anticipation of Rasul Guliev's return'. It further expressed concern that 'some executive authorities were intervening in the campaign in favour of certain candidates, and in some cases have interfered with the electoral process'. The US statement also expressed hope that Azerbaijan would continue its efforts to conduct free and fair elections. (Quoted from Turan news agency, 21 October 2005).

Concerns

While Washington expressed its support for a peaceful scenario for developments in Azerbaijan, and hoped for the political will of the President to conduct free and fair elections, there was no doubt at the level of civil society and within the opposition that the leadership intended to have controlled elections. The opposition was concerned by the degree of the US commitment towards influencing, or preventing, the possibility of the state reacting violently towards the public protests – in response to what was, most probably, going to be another set of fraudulent elections. The positive step forward, as compared to 2003, was found in US policy during the pre-election period, as shown by its statements regarding the necessity of respecting the freedom of assembly. On the other hand, the US appeals made to both parties to 'abstain from violence' provided the Azerbaijani government with an opportunity to use 'mass disorder' as a pretext for employing force to quell public protests.

Non-Governmental Actors

Unlike official representatives, non-governmental actors in the USA had been sending clearer messages to the Azerbaijani government. In May 2005, Freedom House issued recommendations urging the Azerbaijani government to demonstrate its commitment to democratic reform. Freedom House once again called on the government of Azerbaijan to cease its aggressive denial of rights and its violence against opposition activists and political candidates; to allow fair media representation for diverse political views, able to reach a national audience; to permit unfettered activity of civil society in the election run-up and afterwards. Jennifer L. Windsor, executive director of Freedom House, stated: 'The Azerbaijani government must cease trying to silence opposition members, candidates, and journalists, and must ensure that, next month, free and fair elections lay the foundation for the future of democratic progress in Azerbaijan' (Turan, 22 October 2005).

The USA: Post-Election Conclusions

The International Election Observation Mission
The US reaction to the elections was conveyed within the International Election Observation Mission and was backed by the statement of Adam Ereli, State Department spokesman: the 6 November parliamentary elections had been 'an improvement over previous elections in some areas'. However, the USA shared the view of the preliminary assessment of the OSCE Observer Mission that, despite these improvements, the elections had failed to meet several international standards. The decision by the government of Azerbaijan to allow large numbers of candidates to register and provide them with

greater access to the media was praised, as it gave voters 'a real choice on Election Day (...) We are disturbed, however, by credible reports, in selected districts around the country, of major irregularities and fraud that may have disenfranchised voters in those districts. We call on all citizens of Azerbaijan to address complaints about election violations through legal and peaceful channels, and to refrain from violence. We urge the government of Azerbaijan to make allowances for the peaceful freedom of assembly, and to exercise restraint in responding to protests.' Thus, the US State Department spokesperson shared the OSCE conclusions, but also noted some improvements. However, his message did not specify what consequences fraudulent elections might have for the status of US–Azerbaijani relations.

US Congress
The reaction of the representatives of the US Congress was more straightforward. Chairman of the Helsinki Commission, Senator Sam Brownback, stated: 'Unfortunately, the authorities who implemented the election did not pass the test. As is clear from the OSCE assessment, Baku has failed to fully observe its obligations under the Helsinki Final Act, hindering the democratic process in Azerbaijan.' The Helsinki Commission on Security and Co-operation in Europe is a US government agency that monitors the progress of the implementation of the provisions of the 1975 Helsinki Accords. 'The high expectation that the elections would move democratisation forward in Azerbaijan has, regretfully, not been realized,' added Commission Co-Chairman, Rep. Chris Smith. 'There is not even the pretense that the elections results are legitimate', stated Commission Ranking Member, Rep. Ben Cardin: 'It is not at all clear where Azerbaijan goes from here, but I am not optimistic. The international community is clearly going to have to make its displeasure heard.' (From Turan news agency release, 9 November 2005)

Impact of Exit Poll Results
Even though the US assessment was in line with the preliminary conclusion of the International Observation Mission, the major point of reference for its subsequent policy was the result of the exit poll conducted by the PA Consulting Company. The poll revealed six cases of obvious fraud and three cases where there was a strong indication of fraud. This contrasted sharply with the

view of the opposition, which claimed that results in the majority of constituencies had been falsified. Additionally, the opposition reported 21,000 nationwide violations, as well as noting the conclusions of the local observers which
confirmed that the violations were of a mass character. Even the international
observers found 43% of the counting to be 'bad or very bad'. Two consequen-
tial statements by the US Embassy, and later by Assistant Secretary of the
US State Department, Dan Fried, revealed the ultimate forced reconciliation
of Washington's decision on the outcome of the election struggle. The opposition and civil society realised that the scope of external support had been nar-
rowed down.

Internal Responses
Although the Azerbaijani government did not take specific constituencies into
account (this was identified by the USAID-sponsored exit poll as 'fraudulent'),
Washington welcomed the 30 November decision of the Constitutional Court
of Azerbaijan to annul results in five additional constituencies held to have
been affected by electoral fraud. 'These are positive steps, but more needs to
be done', the statement of the US State Department declared, as conveyed
by its spokesman, Sean McCormack, in Washington DC on 2 December. This
statement, along with the speech of the Assistant Secretary of State (at the
Enterprise Institute), Daniel Fried, was generally interpreted as indicating unambiguous support for the government of Azerbaijan This caused deep disappointment among the opposition and in public opinion in general. It was
clear that those ten re-runs would hardly be enough to affect the nature of the
country's new parliament.

Europe

The other influential actor in Azerbaijani elections was Europe and its multilateral institutions. Here there was a difference in the assessments of the
Council of Europe and OSCE on the one hand, and the European Union on
the other, as well as among the various delegations from European states.

Notable Visitors

During the election year, Azerbaijan received frequent visits from representatives of European organisations, the Council of Europe in particular. Aside from the regular visits made by the monitoring committee representatives of PACE (Andreas Gross and Andres Herkel), the Secretary General of the Council of Europe, Terry Davis, came to Azerbaijan in August 2005. He expressed concern about the worsening of the pre-election situation in Azerbaijan, and appealed to the media to abstain from 'black PR'. Davis stressed that, although the presidential decree of 11 May was a positive signal, he was concerned that the relatively quiet June/July pre-election situation had worsened in August. The Coe Secretary genera; touched upon obligations such as freedom of thought and the media, and said that everything was moving very slowly, including the issue of political detainees, which was 'a heavy burden on the shoulders of European–Azerbaijani relations' (*Zerkalo* ,1 September 2005).

The Venice Commission of the CoE, the OSCE and ODIHR

The Venice Commission of the Council of Europe and the OSCE/ ODIHR have worked closely with the Azerbaijani government since Azerbaijan joined the CoE in 2001 and since its ratification of the European Convention on Human Rights and Fundamental Freedoms (ECHR), whose article 3 of Protocol 1 concerns the obligation of states to hold free elections. Representatives of both the OSC and ODIHR have participated in the observation of elections since 2000, and, along with the Venice Commission of the CoE, worked with the Azerbaijani government on improving the Election Code originally adopted on 17 May 2003. It was later amended and adopted by parliament in June 2005, after the release of the 'Joint Recommendations on the Election Code and Electoral Administration in Azerbaijan' by the Venice Commission and OSCE/ODIHR, and the Presidential Decree of 11 May 2005 on '(The) Improvement of Election Practices in the Republic of Azerbaijan'. However, in the Draft Final Opinion of 30 August, the authors concluded that the amendments reflect their recommendations only to a limited degree, in connection with minor and technical issues, and that they do not fully meet OSCE and CoE standards. On 25 October, just a few days before the election, the Azerbaijani president, faced with mounting pressure, issued the second decree (following the first decree of 11 May). This new decree allowed for local NGO participation in observation and instructed that an inking procedure be introduced; provided for administrative and criminal sanctions for violations; and obliged local and central executive authorities to create equal conditions for the freedom of assembly. However, he left the issue of the composition of the election commissions unchanged. This proved that the government stood firm with regard to the most crucial factor: that it intended to provide central control over the elections.

The OSCE and ODIHR Mission

The OSCE/ODIHR deployed their mission on the 5 September, with 18 experts and 30 long-term observers in the capital and 13 regional centres. On Election Day, 6 November, the International Election Observation Mission deployed 617 short-term observers from 42 OSCE participating states, visiting more than half of all polling stations in the country. They observed the polling and vote count in over 2,500 polling stations, as well as in 90 constituency election commissions after the polling stations closed. The group included 62 parliamentarians from the OSCE PA, 51 from the PACE, 12 from the European Parliament and 11 from the NATO PA. On 7 November, the International Observation Mission held a press conference on the results of its observations of the parliamentary elections. The harsh conclusion: 'The 6 November parliamentary elections in Azerbaijan did not meet a number of OSCE commitments, and Council of Europe standards, for democratic elections.' While there were improvements in some respects during the pre-election period, there was evidence of uncertainty concerning key aspects of the process, such as voter registration. Furthermore, the continued restrictions on the freedom of assembly, a fundamental right, marred the campaign period, according to the mission statement.

Voting was generally calm, but during the Election Day process it progressively deteriorated during the counting and, in particular, the tabulation of votes. The preliminary statement had a relatively balanced account of the positive and negative elements of the elections. In 87% of the cases the observers had made positive assessments to the voting, while in 43% of the cases counting was assessed as 'bad and very bad'. Observers witnessed the following: attempts to influence voter choices; unauthorised persons inter-

fering in, or directing, the process; and cases of ballot stuffing. Inking procedures, in particular the checking of voters' fingers for traces of ink, were not
followed in 11% of polling stations visited, with several polling stations not
applying the procedure at all. Domestic observers, and some members of
polling station commissions, were observed being expelled from polling stations. Ambassador Geert-Heinrich Ahrens, Head of the OSCE/ODIHR long-
term observation mission, concluded, 'Having read the presidential decree of
11 May, I had very much hoped for a better election and consequently a more
positive assessment by the International Election Observation Mission. Unfortunately, the results of our observation made this impossible.' The preliminary
report also devoted extensive space to the election campaign (including the
media), criticising its bias towards the official party and pro-government candidates.

This report was visibly tougher than the one on the presidential elections in
2003, which had started with a rather positive remark.: 'The voting on the 15
October 2003 presidential elections in the Republic of Azerbaijan was generally well-administered in most polling stations, but the overall election process
still fell short of the international standards in several aspects.'

This can be compared to the first sentence of the International Election
Observation Mission (IEOM) preliminary conclusion in November 2005:, 'The
6 November parliamentary elections did not meet a number of OSCE commitments and Council of Europe standards and commitments for democratic
elections'. Unlike the assessment of the parliamentary elections in Georgia,
for instance, the introduction did have an assurance that the institutions represented in the IEOM stood ready to support the authorities of Azerbaijan and
conduct fair elections. Furthermore, in the report on the parliamentary elections in Georgia, the international observers questioned 'the willingness and
capacity of the governmental and parliamentary authorities to conduct a
credible election process', whereas in the conclusion about the elections in
Azerbaijan, they praised the 'political will, expressed by the high level authorities'. This was, however, only 'partially implemented by the executives'. This
highlighted that the shortcomings were more a result of bad implementation
than of a lack of political will.

The composition of the OSCE mission at the 2005 election differed from
that at the 2003 presidential elections. During the 2003 presidential elections,

the mission had had more than 100 observers from IDEE (the Institute of Democracy in Eastern Europe). None of these organisations received an invitation in 2005; moreover, Irena Lasota, director of IDEE, was denied a visa by the Azerbaijani authorities. This is attributed to the stricter assessment of the Azerbaijan presidential elections in 2003, rather than the assessment of the mission in general (i.e. the 'special opinion' within the OSCE/ODIHR mission). This time the OSCE had 81 observers from Russia, who also expressed their special opinion – but this was of a quite different nature, criticising the mission for its assessment of Azerbaijani elections, which, it said, were too strict.

All the same, the OSCE/ODIHR-led mission remained one of the most credibly perceived actors in these parliamentary elections. Both the government and the opposition made reference to the report. However, the fact that two actors with opposite claims repeatedly referred to the same report probably indicates that it was too balanced to make a significant effect on the situation. For example, the section of the report which stated that 87% of the voting went well was often referred to by the government, whereas the opposition frequently cited the section which stated that counting in 43% of cases was deemed 'bad and very bad'.

The presidency of the European Union supported the OSCE/ODIHR conclusion and urged the government to investigate the cases of fraud which took place in a large number of constituencies, and to take relevant action. It also appealed to all parties to abstain from violent confrontation.

The Parliamentary Assembly of the Council of Europe

A significant role in the elections was played by the Parliamentary Assembly of the Council of Europe, through the representatives of the monitoring committee. They reported to the PACE on the implementation of Azerbaijan's obligations concerning the provision for free and fair elections. The change in attitude became evident when, visiting Azerbaijan, representatives of the monitoring committee extended the range of regular meetings to the leaders of opposition. This was a way of trying to develop a dialogue between the government and the opposition parties. All three representatives of PACE (Leo Platvoet, Andreas Gross and Andres Herkel) were straightforward in their assessment of the parliamentary elections in Azerbaijan. Gross called them a 'step back' for Azerbaijan. This sharply contrasted with all the international assessments of elections in the previous years, which had referred to them as 'steps forward'. The statements by Gross and Herkel had a significant influence on the perception of public, and the democratic constituency, regarding the position of the West in the Azerbaijani parliamentary elections. Most of the opposition, as well as the non-partisan newspapers and the TV channel ANS, devoted considerable space to interviews with both representatives, and to discussions around their statements and assessments.

The Norwegian Perspective

Similarly, the Norwegian Ambassador to Azerbaijan was openly critical of the elections. He had already gained a reputation as the most principled and consistent promoter of democratic values in the country after the presidential elections in 2003, when he had raised his voice in defence of human rights. The Norwegian government urged the Azerbaijani authorities to punish those who were to blame for the parliamentary elections fraud. According to a statement issued by the Norwegian Embassy and spread by the local news agency Turan on 8 November 2005, 'The Norwegian government deeply regrets that the conduct of the parliamentary elections in Azerbaijan far from satisfied international standards. The elections are a step back for democracy in Azerbaijan.'

The Council of Europe

The Council of Europe (CoE) rebuked Washington for its support of Azerbaijani President Ilham Aliev's regime despite serious allegations of fraud in the recent parliamentary elections. Speaking at a press conference, a high-level delegation from the CoE not only criticised President Aliev and other government authorities, but had harsh words for US President George Bush as well.

Leo Platvoet of the CoE also stated that the Council's impression was that election returns had been declared invalid in several constituencies 'not because there was a lot of fraud, but because the candidate of the opposition won'. Significantly, the CoE representatives indicated the possibility of at least one punitive measure that the body could take: non-recognition of the country's new parliament. 'We will accept the parliament when the elections are not fraudulent', said Platvoet. The CoE delegation also expressed its dismay

with the US State Department's position so soon after the 26 November police crackdown on demonstrators in Galaba Square in Baku.

The EU
A real disappointment for liberal sectors of Azerbaijani society was caused by
the statements by the EU special representative to the South Caucasus region, Heike Talvitiye, who, during his visit to Baku on 22 November 2005,
'positively' assessed the democratic processes in Azerbaijan.

'Before the elections, I said that an evolution in events was possible in
Azerbaijan. Now I have been made certain of that', stated Talvitiye, who said
that he interpreted the November parliamentary elections as '(a) step forward'
as compared with previous elections. At a press conference, Talvitiye did
admit that some voting irregularities 'caused serious concern', and urged
Baku officials to eliminate these shortcomings within the framework of the
law. At a meeting with representatives of the government and the opposition,
he said that all the disputable issues must be resolved – once again, within
the framework of the law. (Turan news agency, 23 November 2005)

Europe: Other Opinions

Along with the joint statement, there were also various other opinions among
Western delegations. When compared to the OSCE/ODIHR statement, the
assessments from the observers of the European Parliament and the NATO
Parliamentary Delegation were softer. The Swedish parliamentarian, Goran
Lindblad, told participants at a Johns Hopkins University teleconference on 7
November: '(the) elections were a sign of a step forward'. Bulgarian observ-
ers gave a positive conclusion, as they had done 2003, and noted Azerbai-
jan's improved electoral process *(Eurasian Daily Monitor,* 17 November 2005,
Vol. 2, No. 215).

The report from the International Crisis Group (ICG) condemned the government of Azerbaijan, stating that the presidential elections in 2003, municipal elections in 2004 and the recent parliamentary elections in Azerbaijan had
been falsified. In order to prevent such incidents in the future, it is necessary,
the report went on to say, to investigate frauds, punish those to blame, and
ensure uniformity within electoral commissions. If the government fails to take

these steps and uses force against peace demonstrators, then sanctions should be imposed on the country.

ICG Caucasus Project Director, Sabine Freizer, told journalists that Ilham Aliev was personally responsible for the conduct of the elections. She added that the world community must exert pressure on the republic. Furthermore, she said, it was also necessary to create a group of ambassadors to work with the government, the opposition, and the CEC, in order to eliminate violations, and noted that similar groups had worked rather effectively in Georgia and Ukraine. Since the ICG was closely involved in the resolution of the conflicts in the Caucasus, some analysts suggested that the harshness of this statement might be interpreted as pressure on the President in order to obtain greater concessions in the negotiations process.

Russia

Russian Involvement
Russia's interest in the parliamentary elections in Azerbaijan in 2005 was more profound than in the previous years. In the context of the three velvet revolutions – which Moscow had perceived as its 'defeat' in the geopolitical competition with Washington – Russia increased its attention to the Azerbaijani elections. Prior to the 2005 elections, it sent several high-ranking representatives to Baku, most notably Sergey Lebedev, head of Russia's Foreign Intelligence Service. It is also worth noting that, against the background of the usual refusal to attend the international meetings held in Yerevan, this time (prior to the elections on 29–30 September) the Deputy Minister of Internal Affairs of Azerbaijan attended a meeting of the interior minister of the CIS in Yerevan (the meetings was led by a Russian minister). The Azerbaijani authorities also made extensive use of the services of political technologists led by Gleb Pavlovskii. It is hardly a coincidence that Vladimir Rushailo, executive secretary of the Commonwealth of Independent States and head of the CIS monitoring delegation, had praised the electoral process ever since his arrival in Baku several weeks prior to the actual vote. Members of the opposition blamed Rushailo for interfering in the domestic affairs of the country. Following the elections, Russia's Ministry of Foreign Affairs declared: 'The elections have passed according to Azerbaijani legislation', and Vladimir Putin

congratulated his Azerbaijani counterpart, Ilham Aliev, on, 'successful parliamentary elections' (Azertaj News Agency, 9 November 2005).

Russian-Led CIS Missions

Russia led the CIS mission, with a total of 640 observers. CIS observers visited 3,087 polling stations; 2,838 were also visited by other observers. The CIS started its mission on 6 October, with headquarters in Baku and four other cities: Gianja, Lenkoran, Nakhichevan and Khachmas.

CIS Conclusions

Unlike OSCE/ODIHR, CIS highly praised the national legislative basis for the election and pre-election situation. The only suggested changes were to Article 46.1, in order to allow to the election commissions to include, within the lists, those who were not on the lists but had a document confirming their residency in the district. They suggested changes to Article 46.1 so as to allow voting before Election Day, and to allow voting with a residency-confirming document for those who were not on the voters' lists.

The CIS conclusion also praised the practice of voters' IDs and the inking procedure, introduced for the first time in Azerbaijan. In a similar manner to the other observers, the CIS observers did not notice violations during the registration of the candidates. However, unlike the Western observers, the CIS did not note any violations of the freedom of assembly or unequal rights of opposition candidate campaigning. Similarly, they ignored irregularities observed by the IEOM regarding access to the electronic media (TV channels). CIS monitoring of the media, from 10 October to 4 November, led to the conclusion that the TV coverage of the election process had been, as a rule, objective and balanced. They stressed, however, that some candidates insulted the honour of their rivals, while some called for civil disobedience and violence. CIS monitors observed cases of local executives interfering in the election in only three districts.

The CIS stressed the fact that, of 47 appeals to sanction a rally by the opposition, 38 received a positive response from the authorities. They blamed the opposition parties for 'aggressiveness' and for creating social-political tension. The CIS also praised the procedure for the filing of complaints and their review in the courts. The opinion refers to 'separate cases' where there were violations of election law.

However, the exit poll was assessed negatively by the CIS, who held that the results of the exit polls could not be taken into account, as the polls had been implemented with serious violations and falsifications. Similarly, the inking procedure was negatively assessed, as it 'complicated the work of the precinct commissions, creating queues, and did not have a quality certificate, confirmed medically.'

CIS and Other International Observers: Comparing Results
The major divergence in the assessments related to the count and tabulation. While the IEOM concluded that the count in 43% of the cases was 'bad or very bad', the CIS observers did not notice any violations. The CIS observers concluded that they did not consider the individual violations to be of a mass character and thus were not seen as affecting the outcome of the elections.

At the request of the Russian Federation, OSCE/ODIHR included 81 Russian experts in the short-term observation mission in Azerbaijan. Some analysts suggested that the presence of the Russian observers in OSCE/ODIHR was aimed at softening the group's final assessment of the election process.

The assessment by Russia's delegation differed from the overall assessment of the elections by OSCE/ODIHR. Furthermore, the Russian issued a separate remark, made by the head of the delegation of the Russian Foreign Ministry, Alexander Chepurin. This statement was far softer than the conclusion of IEOM, and focused on the problems related to the work of ODIHR itself, rather than on the elections as such. It made reference to the fact that no Russian expert had been included in the team of long-tem observers and analysts, and sharply criticised the statement by Alcee Hastings and the OSCE/ODIHR press release as being non-objective. The conclusion expressed hopes that the opinion of Russian observers in OSCE/ODIHR would be taken into account in the final opinion of the mission.

Other Regional Actors

Iran

Iran sent a delegation of 21 observers, led by the former Iranian ambassador to Azerbaijan, Ahad Gazai, currently an advisor to the minister of foreign affairs. The delegation opted for a similar pattern to Russia, lauding the elections and supporting Aliev's party. The Azerbaijan ambassador to Iran, Afshar Suleymani, said that the elections had been democratic and transparent (day.az 8 November 2005). For Iran, relations with the Azerbaijani government are extremely important: as a strategic partner of the USA, Azerbaijan may play an important role in the region in the context of Washington's policy in Iran.

Turkey

Although not openly praising the Azerbaijani elections, the official position of Turkey was also supportive of President Aliev and his policies on the improvement of the electoral process in the country. Although the Azerbaijani opposition has maintained old ties with politicians in Turkey, relations with the authorities seemed to dominate in Turkish foreign policy. There were particular cases of indignation in public TV speeches of members of an organisation close to the government in Turkey, the Marmara Group, who sent 82 observers and praised the elections highly. However, at the societal level, there were appeals for the support of the democratic forces in the country – like that from the Turkish Centre for Strategic Analysis, which stressed the importance of not sacrificing democracy in Azerbaijan for the sake of temporary stability *(Baki Xeber,* 2 November 2005, p. 7).

Assessments by Local Observer Teams

Local NGOs

Local NGOs had been practising election observation in Azerbaijani elections since 1998 and had been active in observing the 1998 and 2000 parliamentary elections. However, after 2000, observation participation of local NGOs with more than 30% of foreign funding was prohibited by law. Despite this, civil society participated in observation on an individual basis in the presidential elections in 2003, and in the municipal elections in 2004.

In October 2005, 10 days prior to the parliamentary elections, a presidential decree lifted the ban on NGO participation in election observation. Altogether the number of local observers, candidates' representatives and lawyers participating in these elections was 17,000. This time, the government registered numerous 'loyal' observers: these were members of the ruling party, whose function was to promote falsifications in favour of the pro-government candidates, rather than observe the integrity of the election process.

A few local NGOs and coalitions participated in the observation of the parliamentary elections. The largest were two coalitions: the Election Monitoring Centre of 14 NGOs and the Consultative Advisory Council for Free and Fair on Elections of 48 NGOs. Together these two covered most of the republic.

All NGOs and coalitions were unanimous in their assessment: violations took place all over republic, that they had a mass character and that they significantly affected the outcome of elections. 'At least at half of the districts should hold by-elections'. The Election Monitoring Centre, which had deployed 2,315 observers in 124 districts, and was led by Anar Mammedly, reported numerous falsifications. 'In the afternoon, the intervention that had taken place during the process of elections was of a consistent, mass and uncontrolled nature', according to a statement of the coalition of the 14 local NGOs at a press conference. They were sponsored by the USAID, NDI and the Norwegian Helsinki Committee.

Similarly, the other coalition of local NGOs, led by Arzu Abdullayeva, reported that the violations had mass character and had significantly affected the outcome of the elections. The appeal issued on 22 November stated that the Co-ordinating Advisory Council For Free and Fair Elections united 48 NGOs and deployed 2,237 observers to monitor the 6 November elections in 80 constituencies. The appeal drew attention to violations of the law that occurred during the elections, and made a statement about voting irregularities. In particular, these were interference in the voting process on the part of the police and executive administration, incorrect lists of electors, the creation of polling stations in military units, and intimidation of voters and vote buying. The Council criticised the Central Election Commission (CEC), which had in fact refused to deal with complaints about violations. The human rights activists and election experts branded the 2005 parliamentary elections 'a failure'. The coalition, in particular, paid attention to the groups vulnerable to manipulation at all elections (the military, refugees and IDPs, and prison inmates). These were extensively used in many constituencies in order to afford victory to the pro-government candidates. Observers noted numerous major irregularities in those districts where the leaders or activists of the opposition were running.

The Institute for Peace and Democracy reported numerous violations in Baku villages to which its observation mission had been extended. Inall, 249 observers in 9 districts reported violations like police violence, arrests and detention of observers and members of the local electoral commissions, the practice of bringing voters to the polling stations by bus, pressuring and campaigning for the government candidates at polling stations, and ballot box stuffing. Institute observers also noted police violence against women. Their observations led to the conclusion that none of the results in the nine districts could be trusted.

Compared to the previous years, there was an increase in the participation of local NGOs in election observation. However, the election monitoring work was complicated by various factors: the ban on the participation of NGOs was lifted only a few days before the election; there was a lack of resources (which in turn prevented the training of civil society representatives); the foreign agencies' status in the eyes of the authorities very often led to pressure and violence against the observers. Yet in some instances there were reports that the authorities' blatant falsifications were deterred by the professional, and consistent, work of local observers. The similarities in the assessments of the election by different coalitions helped to develop an independent, local perspective on the election.

Other Reports

The head of election headquarters of the Azadlyg bloc, Panah Huseyn, reported that there had been a total of 21,104 violations in 113 election districts. He noted that, after the completion of the voting process at 7 pm, the police started to arrest observers and steal boxes from the election points. Concerning violations that took place during the day, Huseyn said there had been a number of cases of interference by the executive organs and votes cast without the practice of marking fingers with ink; instances of pressure being exerted on observers; cases whereby one voter voted for several people; cases of ballot-box stuffing; cases of interference by the police; and instances when the wrong use of boxes was observed.

The leader of Musavat party, Isa Gambar, declared that they had observed 'total falsification', whilst the chairman of the PPFA, Ali Kerimli, declared that the elections did not reflect 'the will of people of Azerbaijan' (6 November 2005).

4. Exit Polls

Exit Polls and Azerbaijan: Remarks

Exit polls are an important tool in determining the degree of election fraud. They have been used to discredit elections in emerging democracies where ruling parties were expected to falsify the outcome of the vote. They can, on the other hand, also be used to validate the outcome where there has been an honest count.

Exit polls were conducted for the first time in Azerbaijan. The country's legislation does not provide for the conduct of the exit poll, so the practice was introduced legally by means of a presidential decree of 11 May 2005.

There were three exit polls during the November parliamentary elections in Azerbaijan, conducted by:

- Edison/Mitofsky – (Mitofsky International, a private US company) with Edison Media Research and CESSI Ltd
- PA Consulting (USAID-financed)
- SAAR poll (owned by Alexander Saar, Estonia).

Mitofsky International conducted the 2004 exit polls for the US media. CESSI, a Moscow firm, has worked with Mitofsky on all the Russian exit polls since 1993. Mitofsky International and SAAR poll covered all the constituencies, except for one, while PA Consulting only 65, randomly chosen. Renaissance Associates, the company that hired Mitofsky International, was a Swiss company, run by a Bulgarian national.

Mitofsky International

Mitofsky hired three local organisations to work with them on the Election Day. Interviewing was divided between the Association for Civil Society Development in Azerbaijan (ACSDA) and the Sociological Research and Socio-Economic Forecasting Centre (QAFQAZ). ACSDA did the interviewing in 90 election districts (or parliamentary districts), and QAFQAZ in the other 35. ACSDA had previously done polling for this client, and QAFQAZ had worked with Vladimir Andreenkov (Mitofsky's Russian partner at CESSI) for years.

Mitofsky also hired another Azerbaijani survey company, SIAR (the Social and Marketing Research Centre), to monitor interviewing. There were 105 monitors covering more than one third of all the sampled locations. According to Mitofsky, the results of the monitoring proved that the local partner, AC-SDA, had done an unsatisfactory job. At midday in a key district, interviewers at thirteen of their sample polling places in the twenty precincts could not be located. Furthermore, many questionnaires simply never arrived at company headquarters – likewise with the results reported by the telephone. This was the case in several Baku districts.

But the greatest challenge was to make the report public. Mitofsky reported that, due to difficulties in relations with their sponsor in making the results of the exit poll known to the public, they were able to display their results only 20 hours later, after the official and the SAAR Poll results were known. According to the Mitofsky exit poll results, independent candidates got 39% of the vote. The government party (YAP) candidates had 32%, the Freedom Bloc, a coalition of three opposition parties, received 14%, with the remainder scattered among various parties. The real differences were in regional support for the YAP. According to the poll, such support appeared weakest of all in the capital, in the centre's neighbouring regions and in the northeast of the country.

PA Consulting

The Agency for International Development (USAID), an arm of the US State Department, sponsored an exit poll in 65 of the 125 districts. PA Consulting Group of Madison, Wisconsin, was the lead organisation.

The experts of the PA consulting company announced that their work followed four principles: anonymity, political neutrality, transparency and professionalism. The data were processed at the Baku centre, with two servers and 32 computers, and the results were planned to be reported twice (first by telephone and then by the lists brought to the Centre). According to information provided by the PA consulting company, CEC selection would be random (on a computer lottery basis).

SAAR Poll

There was another exit poll, by the Estonian firm SAAR Poll, apparently sponsored by the Centre for Regional Development in Azerbaijan (directed by Chingiz Ismailov). According to Mitofsky himself, the same people who sponsored their exit poll also were involved with the SAAR Poll.

On 7 November, Andrius Saar, head of SAAR Poll, held a press conference. It was opened by the chief of the Regional Development Centre, Chingiz Ismailov, who stated that 20 representatives of SAAR poll had conducted an exit poll at 1,043 PECs of the 124 CECs. Every fifth one was surveyed, and a total of 800 people were covered in 124 districts. According to SAAR, it was difficult to conduct an exit poll in a country with no experience of it, but they expressed satisfaction with the results. Twelve representatives had been sent to six regions: Goycay, Ismailly, Gianja, Lenkoran, Ali-Bairamly and Saatly.[1] Ismailov did not disclose the inviting party or the source of financing.

Commentary

There was considerable controversy regarding the exit poll companies. The media generally gave credibility to the USAID (or PA Consulting-led) exit poll, even though it was funded by the US government, an open supporter of stability and the current Azerbaijan government. The United States was also known to have urged the issue of fair elections to President Aliev.

Initially, there was concern relating to the presence of Mitofsky International, as it was supposedly hired by the government with an unknown source of financing, but also the activities of PA Consulting activities occasioned certain doubts.

Biased Procedures
Although the credibility of PA Consulting was highly rated, there were concerns about its selection of constituencies (and the doubtful transparency of

---

1   *Baki Xeber*, 8 November 2005, p. 14.

the process of selection, which had left the opposition leaders in the most crucial constituencies out of the coverage); the presence and participation of relatives of the local administration in the conduct of the exit polls; the confusion of data and the delayed appearance of the results on the website.

The practice of not selecting the districts where the leading representatives of the opposition had a high chance of winning became a subject of discussions. According to Rauf Arifoglu, 'society does not consider it to be normal that the most popular leaders, professionals, and prominent intellectuals were left out of the CEC exit polls. It is most probable that this was done with intervention of the government, and that those CECs will be covered by exit polls conducted by the companies invited by the government.'[2] Further: 'The US company announced the constituencies where it will conduct an exit poll. Amongst these, none have the most promising Azadlyg candidates'. As to the impact that excluding these districts may have had on the situation, Arifoglu said 'it will untie the authorities' hands'. Among questionable aspects of the PR Consulting activities were, as reflected in the media: excessive finances at their disposal for the conduct of exit poll; badly trained contractors; and confused results, as well as late publication on the website (*Realniy Azerbaijan*, 18 November 2005, p. 6). Many observers believed that random selection of electoral districts, made in the presence of journalists and NGOs, would have lent credibility to the exit polls.

The public's perception, hopes and expectations of the PA Consulting Company had significantly weakened by Election Day. The opposition and civil society did not trust the partners of the PA Consulting Group, Georgian GORBI or local Sorgu companies. A typical example of the lack of transparency in the conduct of both the election and the exit poll is Constituency 80 (Fizuli) polling station no. 20. The chairman of the commission was a member of the ruling party (YAP), Valida Ibrahimova. The exit poll was conducted by her husband Kerem Zeynalov, while her son was an exit poll supervisor at polling station no.25.

---

2   *Baki Xeber*, 256, 2 November 2005, p. 11.

Limitations

Exit polls can test violations only on Election Day, but not the effect of viola-tions during the pre-election campaign – which in the Azerbaijan case in-cluded the intimidation of voters, vote buying, and excessive use of adminis-trative resources. According to representative of the PACE monitoring com-mittee, Andres Herkel, violations were found in more than 40% of the cases on Election Day alone. There were many violations in the pre-election cam-paign period as well: people withdrew their candidature under pressure, while some candidates were invalidated by courts.[3]

After Election Day, the US Embassy issued a statement that the results of the exit poll were available at their WebPages. It also stated that the exit poll had been by both the government and the opposition parties. Apparently, in a move to address public criticism, the embassy had to confirm the four princi-ples of the conduct of an exit poll (political neutrality, transparency, anonym-ity, and professionalism), and that the exit polls had been conducted under multiple control, so the influence of 'personalities' was excluded. PA Consult-ing disclosed six cases of obvious fraud, and three cases where there was a strong suggestion of fraud. In all nine cases the exit poll disproved the offi-cially announced results. Contrary to the announced winner from the ruling party (or its loyal independents), it confirmed the victory of the Azadlyg bloc in seven districts, the YeS bloc in one district, and an independent in another one. According to exit poll experts the identification of fraud in those districts does not mean that the exit polls confirms the lack of fraud in the other 56 dis-tricts and says nothing about the 60 districts covered by the exit poll.

Exit Polls and Official Results: A Comparison

The divergence with the official results was as follows: in the case of the Mi-tofsky poll, 16%; SAAR Poll, 12%; and 17% according to the poll conducted by PA Consulting. The results of the exit polls conducted by two of the com-panies, Mitofsky and SAAR poll, in 124 constituencies, did not coincide in 25 constituencies. The official results coincided with all three of the other exit polls in only 33 constituencies. The results of all three exit polls were reported

---

3   *Azadlyg,* 8 November 2005, p. 4.

on their websites only after the official data were announced.[4] In general, none of the results of the exit polls were perceived as credible by the public.

---

4   *Realniy Azerbaijan*, 18 November 2005, p. 6.

5. International Assessment and Exit Polls: The Internal Responses

The Authorities

Initial Resistance

The government had taken a tough stance during negotiations over the legal parameters set to underpin the conduct of the elections. Most improvements from the government came as a result of negotiations and pressure from local and international actors, and were of a technical character. The government consistently resisted any major changes that would weaken the ruling elite's grip on power. At the third congress of the 'Yeni Azerbaijan' party (YAP), in March 2005, for instance, Ramiz Mekhtiyev said that the democratic processes in Azerbaijan had been well thought through, had been developing successfully and that the country had been integrating into Europe. Mekhtiyev, head of the presidential administration (and considered to be a key person in the design of the elections), said that the government did not consider it necessary to change the principles governing the formation and membership of the election commissions. The present election commissions had been formed on the basis of the recommendations of the Venice Commission and OSCE, so 'we do not see any necessity to change them'.[5]

As to the harsh criticisms in the OSCE conclusions concerning the elections, Mazahir Panahov, CEC chairman, requested that this issue not 'be exaggerated', because international organisations usually 'do not praise positive moments, they focus on shortcomings'. On the whole, he said, 'the elections were transparent and democratic'. According to him, the official results coincide with the results of the American PA Consulting exit poll by 83%.[6] In cases out of every 65, there were 6 obvious cases of fraud and 3 strong suggestions of fraud).

---

5   *Turan*, 28 March 2005.
6   *Turan*, 7 November 2005.

Presidential Response
The relatively strict assessment by the International Election Observing Mission caught President Aliev by surprise. According to the head of the international relations department of the presidential administration, N. Mamedov, the President was too nervous to go out to journalists and comment on the statement of the IEOM. He only partially acknowledged local and international criticism by saying that irregularities had taken place in a few districts, and that his government would take serious steps to address shortcomings.[7] At the opening of the newly elected parliament, President Ilham Aliev stated: '(The) Council of Europe does not consist of only Gross and Herkel.' In most interviews, representatives of the official power would refer to the figure of 87% (as mentioned in the preliminary report by the OSCE/ODIHR) as proof of the insignificant number of violations. After the election, the government strengthened its PR campaign in the main European organisations. However, the pre-election situation showed that the greater pressure did at least make the government give up on its resistance to the introduction of the inking procedure, as well as allowing the participation of local NGOs in election observation. It seemed that the government preferred to make concessions on relatively 'safe' issues (safe for the existing power monopoly), while remaining firm on the most crucial aspects of the reforms.

Utilising the 'Democracy' Issue
There was a rather standard continuation of the tradition that had been laid down by President Heidar Aliev: the reforms were skilfully used, under the façade of democratisation, in order to further centralise and monopolise power. This was illustrated in the reaction from President Ilham Aliev to the criticism of the international observers and results of an exit poll. As early as two days after the elections, he issued a decree instructing that the people who had violated the law on Election Day should be punished. In accordance with this presidential instruction, the local heads of the executive power of three districts were dismissed, and the results in four districts were invalidated.

---

7   RFE/RL 7 November 2005.

According to copies of the protocols received by local observers in three districts, the opposition candidates were the leaders (and, in one area, an independent). In violation of the law, the authorities did not re-count ballots, but simply annulled the results. Furthermore, 460 polling stations where the opposition had a clear victory were eliminated. Of more than 500 complaints submitted by the opposition and independent candidates to the CEC, half were not even considered, while the other half were declined, as were more than 40 complaints filed to the Court of Appeals.

Cementing the Outcome: the Constitutional Court Decision
On 1 December, the Constitutional Court approved the overall results of Azerbaijan's 6 November parliamentary elections. The court invalidated results in six constituencies, including one where the chairman of the major opposition, the Popular Front (PFPA) party, Ali Kerimli, had run. Prior to the decision, Kerimli had been announced the winner from his constituency, along with five other candidates, including another PFPA executive (Gulamhuseyn Alibeyli) and the editor-in-chief of the Azerbaijan newspaper parliamentary publication, *Bahtiyar Sadigov*. Altogether, the CEC and the high court invalidated the results of ten constituencies.

The decision of the Constitutional Court only confirmed the official results of the parliamentary elections. It was made early, although representatives of the monitoring Committee PACE, Gross and Herkel planned their visit before the decision day. It was not a coincidence that the Constitutional Court's session hurriedly took place before their arrival. In this regard, the statement of the US State Department looked as though it was hasty support for the Azerbaijani government. Only one of the nine districts revealed by the USAID-sponsored exit poll as likely to be fraudulent coincided with those in which the authorities chose to punish their representatives for election law violations. Nevertheless, this move caused an immediate appraisal from the US State Department and some other international organisations. For local civil society actors, the move was seen as lip service of the authorities in reaction to criticism, and a way of initiating yet another crackdown on the opposition. Civil actors argued that there was no need to cancel the polling results in the districts and precincts where all that was needed was a recount.

The Constitutional Court decision took away the last hope of both Azerbaijani society and of Western diplomats, who had tried to convince the opposition that they should wait for the Constitutional Court decision in order for justice to be restored concerning election frauds. The European diplomats had
expected that a greater number of complaints would be reviewed and solved
positively.

Other Reactions
In the opinion of civil society and the opposition (which was shared by the
representatives of the Council of Europe), the authorities deliberately targeted
and cancelled the results in those districts and precincts where, according to
the acquired protocols, opposition candidates had a clear victory. Similarly,
the local heads of executive power were punished where they had failed to
provide a smooth win for the desired authority candidate. The real reason for
the punishment was widely interpreted as the executives' 'botched job' in
promoting the 'right candidates', rather than for violations of the law through
interference in the election process. Another argument, disproving the genuine intentions of the authorities, was that no punishment was applied in many
other cases of violations: in particular, at the numerous military polling stations that had been established on the territory of military units, in violation of
the election law. The military units were used extensively as part of the manipulation in all previous elections, and 'helped' to win the elections by many
'appointed' candidates.

The encouraging approval of the official post-election reaction to the criticism of elections by some international actors, except for the representatives
of the monitoring committee of PACE, affected the behaviour of the ruling
elite. The government welcomed the US Embassy statement. Ali Hasanov,
head of the presidential administration's political department, said that the
government of Azerbaijan was satisfied with the US' 'constructive evaluation'
of the parliamentary election results. 'We [the government] consider the US
Embassy statement (to be) a positive assessment of the parliamentary elections', Hasanov told APA news agency on 3 December. Even after the results
of the exit poll had been disclosed, showing major irregularities in certain districts, the newly 'elected' parliamentarians were not discouraged. In December, in an interview with the ANS TV channel, former head of the foreign rela-

tions committee, Samed Seidov (who had been re-elected, according to the exit poll, in fraudulent circumstances) assured the audience that no serious sanctions were awaiting Azerbaijan at the January PACE session. To support his ideas, he used Turkey as an example, stating that, despite the military coups, that country had managed to join the Council of Europe just few decades later.

The effect of the 'priority of stability' agenda on the policies which foreign states had with Azerbaijan (including Russia's uncritical support for the incumbent regime) was demonstrated at one of the post-election rallies of opposition. Despite all previous international appeals to the government that it should respect the freedom of assembly, the authorities responded with an excessive use of force at a peaceful rally of the opposition on 26 November. This resulted in dozens of people being wounded – among them, women, and children and old people. Prior to the planned end of the rally, and without warning, the government employed internal troops, along with its special riot police, using batons, dogs, tear gas, and water cannons against the protesters.

The Opposition

The opposition welcomed the IEOM and OSCE/ODIHR conclusion regarding the parliamentary elections. However, despite the harsh language, Western actors seemed keen to avoid the revolutionary scenario, and for this reason the Baku-based foreign diplomats initiated a dialogue between the opposition and authorities behind closed doors. In the evening of 6 November, the head of the election headquarters of the Azadlyg bloc, Panah Huseyn, announced that, over the country, 21,000 violations had been observed, and recommended that the results in the majority of districts should be invalidated.[8].Human rights activists and members of Azadlyg called for the creation of a national resistance movement.

Assessing the results of the parliamentary election, the leader of the Musavat Party, Isa Gambar, said that the electors had voted for changes in the republic, but that the transition from an authoritarian regime to a democ-

---

8   *Bakinskiye Vedomosti,* 12 November 2005.

racy was impossible without the support of the world community. In an interview with local media, he praised the international assessments immediately after the elections, like those made by the OSCE/ODIHR, the USA and Norway. He noted that the authorities had become more skilful in hiring people from abroad to observe and legitimise elections, but the OSCE remained the most important body in terms of election assessment, so the results of an exit poll were not of particular importance.[9]

The position of the USA, which was seen as crucial to the outcome of the struggle of the democratic and non-democratic forces in other former Soviet states (as was expressed in a series of statements), came as a disappointment, in particular regarding the reaction to the decision of the Constitutional Court on 1 December. The US Embassy statement, issued on 2 December , congratulated the Constitutional Court for the cancelling the election results in the ten constituencies, and expressed optimism about working with the newly elected members of parliament. It urged the government 'to press ahead with the prosecution of those who were engaged in fraud', and called on police to 'respect the rights of peaceful, free assembly'. The statement also reminded the authorities about the need to hold fresh elections in the ten constituencies, in accordance with international standards.

The Need for Answers

In a statement issue on 3 December, leaders of Azadlyg and the opposition (the Liberal and National Independence Parties) expressed their 'surprise and regret concerning the hasty welcoming statement by the USA about the Constitutional Court's decision' and called it a 'double standards approach' as compared to the elections in Georgia and Ukraine. 'We regret that the US President and State Department did not fulfil their pre-election declarations, and dealt a heavy blow to the democratic process in Azerbaijan.'

The opposition leaders contacted the US Embassy for an explanation of the statement. On 7 December, Ambassador Reno Harnish met with PFPA Chairman Ali Kerimli, Musavat Party Chairman Isa Gambar, Democratic Party of Azerbaijan First Deputy Chairman Sardar Jalaloglu and Liberal Party

---

9   *Realniy Azerbaijan*, 11 November 2005.

Chairperson Lala Shovket. According to some sources, Reno Harnish tried to convince the opposition to agree to enter the parliament.

The media devoted extensive space to the discussion surrounding Dan Fried's statement at the American Enterprise Institute after this decision. Mr Fried had stated that (as was conveyed through a local newspaper) '(the) elections in Azerbaijan and Kazakhstan were not free and fair, but neither were they totally devoid of seriousness. There is a big difference between imperfect elections and a parody of elections.' He also stressed that both election exit polls gave the full impression of the nature and scale of the elections. Dan Fried conveyed the message that, besides moral transparency, tactical realism should be taken into account. He said that this would allow for the gradual and consistent achievement of the US objectives, and for cooperation with the states which make a move in the right direction.[10] This was a confusing statement which contradicted the previous US statements regarding the elections. All this was perceived with irony among the opposition and civil society.

Contributions from the Opposition's Media Community

The newspapers of the leading opposition discussed US foreign policy and the US role in the election. Local analysts questioned whether the Pentagon decision to set aside USD 300 million towards the promotion of its international image would help to reach the overall objective. This was applied to the case of Azerbaijan, where the first blow to the US image took place after 2003 presidential election. During the past decade, the democratic camp in Azerbaijan had established friendly relations with America. However, the USA began closing its eyes to the suppression of democracy in 2003. This caused disappointment among the population, who felt that ten years of hopes had been crushed. This damaged not only the USA, but also its supporters. The next betrayal took place in 2005. During, and in particular after, the election, the 'US manipulative approach, and most terribly, welcoming support of the fraudulent actions of the government, was met with indignation in society'. This was especially shocking, the author stressed, following the statements

---

10   *Paytaxt Sabah,* no. 63, 17 December 2005, p. 9 'The US "non-serious" approach to the elections'.

from Washington, which declared that, 'We will give freedom to those who want it'. In the journalist's opinion, it was hard to believe that the US image would improve in Azerbaijan in the near future, even if millions of dollars were being spent on that purpose. As long as Ilham Aliev remained in power, the USA would always be perceived as his supporter.

Deputy chief of the Musavat Party, Sulhaddin Akber, said that the US attitude to democracy and democratic values in the Karabagh conflict, and the 907 amendment, had been crucial in these relations. The 907 amendment is an amendment to the Freedom Support Act, adopted by the US Congress in 1992, prohibiting any aid to the Azerbaijani government because of its conflict with Armenia The fact that Washington did not support the democratic forces or the democratic processes in the elections deepened the negative image of the USA in the country. This was especially the case during the last parliamentary elections, when the USA did not stand by the people's striving for freedom, and there was an inconsistency in the statements made at a high level. This created some serious questions. He also stressed that it meant a big blow to the democratic forces in Azerbaijan. 'The US tried to affect our authorities in meetings behind closed doors, but it did not work. Thus, in this competition, Russia won' (*Yeni Musavat,* no.323, 18 December 2005, p. 6. 'America's fault: by whom and how big?).

Rauf Arifoglu, editor of *Yeni Musavat,* bluntly stated that the USA bears special responsibility for the defeat of the democracy in Azerbaijan. 'We were expecting serious steps from the USA. However, the USA took opposite stance: it gave priority to its oil and other interests. This action will have a high price for both the USA and democracy in Azerbaijan.' The editor reminded his readers of the significant US contribution in maintaining the Aliev dynasty. He suggested that this was due to a religious factor: that the USA has different attitudes to democracy in Christian and in Muslim states. 'It is clear that the USA considers us as being alien and does not include us in the world community of democrats'. He also stressed that hopes of the US influence could even be found in Baku villages, which are considered to be the most conservative area, with a significant religious influence. If the USA could help to prevent falsification of elections, it would increase its reputation in other Muslim countries. But now such a hope is over. The conclusion is that, 'if one wants to win or get support of the USA, one should be strong. And one needs to work permanently inside the country, regardless of the position of the USA, because this is a necessary element of winner'. [11]

To the public, the effect of the OSCE preliminary statement was significant. The newspaper *Bakinskiye Vedomosti* wrote that, after the OSCE statement (which it called the 'slap in the face' of the authorities), the government had to cancel results in several CECs; it did this in the in 31st, for instance, where Ali Kerimli had been announced a winner.

There was an obvious discrepancy between how the foreign and local observers perceived the election, the latter being more negative than the former. The government cancelled, and reviewed, its results in only a very limited number of districts. This contrasted with the results of the observation missions of the local organisations, and even the OSCE, which noted a greater number of violations (43%), far from the numbers given by opposition. This made the opposition resort to rallies as a means of pressure on the government. After the opposition bloc Azadlyg appealed to the people to come out on 9 November, the government took measures to block the meeting. Entrance from the regions to Baku was closed. Security in government buildings was strengthened with armoured vehicles and troops. By order of the Office of the President office (as conveyed by the rector), students and teachers in the Baku State University, as well as budgetary organisations, and state infrastructure, were warned not to attend the meetings.

Not unlike the official media, the opposition newspapers referred to the OSCE statement as a means of justifying and legitimising the opposition's claims that the elections were unfair. They did this by referring to a published OSCE statement under the title, 'The opposition has a right and the grounds to protest the elections' or 'OSCE did not recognise the legitimacy of the falsified elections'.[12]

Possibly the most gloomy conclusion was given in *Baki Xeber.* 'The leadership proved that it cannot change. There are two ways ahead: either shut our eyes to the elimination of the state, or to stand up for the struggle. Who can believe that Rasul Guliev, Isa Gambar, or Ali Kerimli, lost the elections? They would beat Ilham Aliev ten times over in a fair competition. Apparently the

---

11   *Realniy Azerbaijan,* 18 November 2005, p. 5.
12   *Baki Xeber,* 8 November 2005, p. 4.

West understands all that its position, regarding the elections, will show its sincerity regarding democracy.'

Another newspaper, *Azadlyg*, wrote extensively about the international assessment, their perception and the effect on the government (on 8 November 2005, p. 10). According to this article, the assessment of the elections by the IEOM was adequate, and was a serious blow to the image of Azerbaijan in Europe and its prospects of integration; '(A) precise assessment was given in the Azerbaijani elections. They did not respond to the European standards. The feudal thinking of the Azerbaijan government prevents it from entering the European gates.' The newspaper also discussed the minor effect that the assessment and exit poll had on official policies, asserting that, over time, instead of improving practice of elections, the government had been perfecting its falsification skills. It also stressed the dangerous trend of growing bureaucratic indifference to the image of Azerbaijan that was being formed in the West.

The West: Friend or Foe?

The statements by the representatives of the monitoring committee PACE, Gross and Herkel, acquired even greater importance in society after the disappointment caused by the USA's expression of its satisfaction with the decision of the Constitutional Court. The newspapers quoted their assessments, as well as the possibility of having a discussion of the issue of the Azerbaijan delegation's mandate at PACE.

This came as an indication of the West's insistence regarding its declared values – particularly important because of the softness and inconsistency of elections assessment in Azerbaijan. This has characterised the overall post-Soviet policy, and position of, the European states and the USA. It has tended to create the following impression, as stated by one of the opposition leaders in an ANS TV interview on 16 December 2005: 'We finally understood that the Western policies were blocking democracy development in Azerbaijan'. There has been the growing impression that the perceived change in the US policy (on the parliamentary elections) could have negative long-term consequences for American influence in Azerbaijan. 'People will simply stop trusting their assurances about their [US] solidarity with those who are fighting for freedom', wrote *Zerkalo*'s Rauf Mirgadirov on 6 December. According to many opposition activists and political analysts, along with local liberals, the West has also lost in these elections

6. Conclusions

Perceiving Different Viewpoints

The opinions delivered by the Russian, Iranian, CIS and Turkish observation missions regarding the conduct of the parliamentary elections were perceived as giving political support for the government. This went along with the expectations of society. Since 2003, the people of Azerbaijan have observed open support for the government from the side of all the regional actors, so they were not surprised by these conclusions. The conclusions made by the states and organisations have not been perceived by society as being credible, and thus have not had independent political significance.

In contrast, the opinion of the observing missions of the USA and Europe were taken seriously by all actors (the government, opposition, civil society), for the reasons mentioned in the introduction.

The public perception was that the government had made a deal with the regional actors, including Turkey and Georgia, while Europe and the USA had managed to combine their principles and interests in their assessment of the elections.

US and European Responses Analysed

Compared to the presidential elections, when Richard Armitage congratulated Ilham Aliev with the victory via a telephone call even before the official results were announced, with the parliamentary elections the US position was more balanced. Washington's official position in the Azerbaijani elections was crucial, but inconsistent. While it had been sending encouraging signals throughout the pre-election year, the substance of its assessment changed significantly after the decision of the Constitutional Court. The new standpoint contradicted its earlier opinions. It was obvious that, because of the multiple agendas and diverse interests, the USA and Europe had limited levers of influence on the Azerbaijani government, for fear of losing out in dialogue in other important areas like security and energy. Given the announced intent of the Azeri government to conduct an honest election this time round, the opportunity of providing the election with credibility was presumably a factor in the funding of the USAID poll.

Within the European camp, conclusions also differed. The most consistent were given by OSCE/ODIHR and PACE, while visibly softer views were given by the EU and the NATO PA. However, because of Europe's institutional ties with Azerbaijan, and various sanctions at its disposal, Europe has greater levers of influence in the country's democratisation process. It is also clear that the major regional powers do not want to spoil relations with the Azerbaijani government, due to the current high level of economic, energy, and security co-operation – so most of them have accepted the election results.

Exit Polls

As has been explained, Azerbaijani legislation does not contain provisions for the conduct of exit polls. This resulted in the respective margins of error and statistical discrepancy. The legislative basis for conducting the exit poll was given in the Presidential decree on 11 May. The exit polls were of limited significance and seemed to serve as tool to confirm the legitimacy of the election results. Unlike Georgia and Ukraine, where the exit polls had showed the winner to be the opposition candidates, and thus undermined the legitimacy the incumbent regime, in Azerbaijan all three exit polls indicated only a limited number of cases of obvious fraud, publicly confirming the overall legitimacy of the election results. Shortcomings in the work of the exit poll companies in these elections prevented the practice from serving as a credible instrument of election assessment. The exit polls did not substantially increase the transparency of the process, as they managed only to address violations that took place on Election Day itself. Instead, it served more as a tool to legitimise the status quo. There was no transparency in the choice of a local partner, or the choice of the districts, so all districts with opposition activists were excluded. Moreover, and the results of the exit polls were not made public until after a period of delay, and later than publication of the official results.

There were also discrepancies in both the observations of the local observers and the polls conducted before the elections. Some showed the opposition bloc leading the race. It is clear that an exit poll which had government financing (whether local or foreign) would not be free from the influence of a particular state's agenda and interests. This was the case with all three exit polls, one of which was supported by the US government, and the two others presumably supported by the Azerbaijani government. The US-sponsored exit poll had a limited effect or influence on the government, which, in its reaction to the international criticism, did not take into account, for instance, of specific constituencies that had been marked by the USAID poll as fraudulent. Instead, it targeted those where the opposition had a clear victory, by cancelling the results instead of ordering a recount.

Explaining the Behaviour of the Ruling Regime

The behaviour of the ruling regime can be explained by a few factors. Members of the regime perceive the democracy agenda as less important in their relations than other agendas like security, conflict resolution or energy.

Reactions to the USA

The US assessment of election, as an independent actor from the International Election Observation Mission, was perceived as rather supportive of the incumbent regime. The fact that, in an attempt to address the shortcomings of the elections (because of the strict assessment by the IEOM) the government did not take into account the results of the exit polls of the observers (or rather, took them into account only formally), showed that it was confident of Western support in any case. This confidence was also based on the recognition that the Azerbaijan leadership is valuable for Russia, who worked closely with the government throughout the election period. In addition, the divergence of interests found in Ukraine and Georgia concerning support for the political forces between Russia and the USA (and Europe) did not exist in Azerbaijan. This was because the government was a strategic partner of the USA through its anti-terrorist coalition and its being a reliable energy source, and had been working together with Western mediators in conflict resolution. However, the more consistent position of such European institutions as the Council of Europe, as compared to the US official position in the Azerbaijani elections, gave a positive image of Europe as a more genuine supporter of the declared principles and values. The sustainability of this positive image of the CoE will depend upon the how consistent its reaction to the Azerbaijani elections remains.

A Final Note on International Assessments

The post-election situation in Azerbaijan demonstrated the effect which the international assessments and differing state positions had on developments. It is highly probable that, if the ruling elite had been the least bit hesitant in its use of force against the demonstrators, the numbers of participants would have swelled, taking into account the scale of dissatisfied population, and the scenario would have been quite different. The international conclusions send important signals to society, empowering certain trends and influencing power centres. If the Azerbaijani government had to face tough sanctions from the side of international community, it would restrict its practice of resorting to the use of force against opposition rallies. In the case of Azerbaijan, the real interests of some critical actors, including the USA, Russia, and to some degree, Europe, did affect the nature of the signals that they were sending to the leadership of country regarding democracy.

Society was disappointed by the West's inconsistency in its promotion and support of democratic values, while the Council of Europe, and certain individual countries, such as Norway, remained the last hope for the Azerbaijani liberals. The deepest scepticism and disappointment was caused by the position of the USA, and this may act to undermine its influence in the country. The international assessments of the elections were perceived as more objective as compared to the previous years, but still did not reach the level of local expectations, particularly in comparison with the position taken by the West in states like Georgia and Ukraine. The gap between the assessment by local and some foreign observers, if continued, might also lead to the alienation of society from those states. Most importantly, observers noted a trend in public perceptions: the people feel that there is a consensus, or conspiracy, between the local ruling elite and the Western actors, in imitating rather than actually promoting democratisation.

The consistent position of the Council of Europe as to Azerbaijani elections may not only be of crucial importance to democratisation, it will also inevitably affect Europe itself. Conversely, if there is inconsistency in Europe's stand regarding its core values, and if it avoids taking action over non-implementation of obligations, this will degrade the quality of European standards and weaken Europe's position in Azerbaijan as well as in the region more generally.

II FRAMEWORKS FOR ELECTION OBSERVATION IN AZERBAIJAN: INSTITUTIONAL IMPROVEMENTS, BUT LITTLE IMPACT?

Ulvi Amirbekov

1. Introduction

Key Developments

In Soviet Azerbaijan, as in all countries with a totalitarian regime, the imple-mentation of public observation during the election period was practically an impossible exercise because the conduct of the election itself was not based on democratic principles. Even though some regulations in the legislation were seen as guaranteeing the right to observe the elections, in practice the implementation of these regulations always failed and they carried a declara-tive character only. As in the entire Soviet empire, the election process was under the full control of a single party. Elections were held without alterna-tives and the results were usually falsified according to the demands of the time.

This article outlines key legal developments in the sphere of election law and portrays the evolution of election observation in Azerbaijan since 1991. It is argued that the importance of election observation in Azerbaijan has grown, but is still facing serious constraints.

The Recent Historical Context

According to most domestic and international observers,[1] the 1992 presidential elections that brought Abulfaz Elchibey into power in Azerbaijan were reasonably free and fair. However, no elections held since then have met either
of these criteria. From the time President Heidar Aliev came to power, all
elections have seen high levels of fraud and manipulation aimed at engineering a suitable outcome. They have received harsh criticism from the international community and domestic opposition alike,[2] and have failed to provide a
level playing field for all the political forces in the country. Due to widespread
fraud during the elections, the political parties in the country have failed to
recognise each other's interests. Instead, they have focused on antagonism
and mutual insults, leading to a high level of distrust and political polarisation
on both sides.

And yet, Azerbaijan's electoral system can be said to be a stable one: all
elections of the past thirteen years have been conducted on time, without delays or postponements. Prior to 1993, the electoral system had operated on a
rather chaotic basis, with presidential elections in 1991, 1992 and 1993 as
well. However, since 1993, parliamentary, municipal, and presidential elections have taken place on a regular basis, as stipulated in the Constitution.
Both the public and the political parties know when to expect the next elections, and this allows them to be better prepared.

New Election Laws

Initial Post-Independence Additions
After gaining independence, Azerbaijan declared its firm commitment to democratic principles, and took its first steps on the way to establishing a democratic, constitutional state, governed by the will of the people and the rule
of law. Early in this process, Azerbaijan undertook a fundamental change

---

1   Evison, Joanna. Elections *Azerbaijani Presidential Elections: A Presidential Choice in*
    Azerbaijan, at: www.democracy-az.net/elections by:
    http://ourworld.compuserve.com/HOMEPAGES/USAAZERB/341.htm
2   See OSCE/ODIHR election reports on Azerbaijan at: http://www.osce.org/odihr-
    elections/14352.html

aimed at the democratisation of society: the introduction of the legislation necessary to establish a democratic election system. The parliament passed laws on presidential (in 1998), parliamentary (in 1995), and municipal elections (in 1999), as well as a law on the work of the Central Election Commission. In this sense, the electoral system was always operating on a solid legislative basis. However, these laws have been the subject of heated debates, as they are riddled with gaps and contradictions and have created obstacles to the participation of political parties in elections. One issue actively debated during these years was the status and role of domestic and international observers in the election process.

The Development of the Status of Election Monitors
The status of election observers was relatively broadly classified in the Law on Elections (as adopted by the *Milli Majlis* [Parliament] on 12 August 1995). For the first time this issue was given proper attention; and, in comparison with other election laws, this resulted in a more systematic approach towards observation. Unfortunately, this law, like its predecessor, was unable to fully address the issue and ensure that the participation of observers in elections followed international standards and best practices. For example, the law did not consider the possibility of a non-partisan organisation conducting election observation in the territory of the whole country. According to the legal requirements, monitoring on such a scale was possible only for the political parties represented in the elections. Not surprisingly, the conclusions and the observations of these institutions always had a one-sided character. The 1995 parliamentary elections clearly showed this: election observation reports produced by the political parties contesting in the race contradicted each other.

After the parliamentary elections, a top issue of debate was election observation, with a more inclusive approach towards institutions responsible for observation, and the participation of independent and non-partisan bodies in this process. As a result of the public debates and of pressure from the international community, this issue found legal expression in legislation adopted after the elections. In the Law on the Elections of the President of the Republic of Azerbaijan in 1998,[3] election observation issues were approached in a broader and more democratic manner. Further improvement came with the presidential decrees and in the regulations adopted by the CEC in connection with the implementation of the law. In this law, and in corresponding orders and regulations, the circle of observers was more broadly defined than in the previous law. According to these acts, not only persons participating in elections, but also public organisations, trade unions and political parties not represented in the current elections were granted the right to observe elections. A basis was also provided for independent organisations to conduct election monitoring in the territory of the whole country. Furthermore, the rights and duties of observers were broadly described in these acts.

The Law of the Azerbaijan Republic on Municipal Elections, adopted on 2 July 1999, further improved the status of observers in the electoral process, and provided a real legal basis for the active participation of observers in elections. In comparison with the previous laws, the new provisions placed an obligation on every single observer appointed by any domestic organisation and intending to observe elections to obtain CEC accreditation.

---

3   The Law on Elections of the President of the Republic of Azerbaijan, 9 June 1998.

2. Elaboration of the Unified Election Code

External Political Conditions

Council of Europe Membership
On 17 January 2001, Azerbaijan joined the Council of Europe (CoE). Most Azerbaijanis were very supportive of the decision to join this pan-European institution, which they felt would support their newly independent state in developing its own democratic institutions. Indeed, in order to become a member of the Council of Europe, many standards must be met, and it was hoped that these would facilitate Azerbaijan's path to democracy. The Council of Europe provides a certain amount of leverage in order to help, encourage and scrutinise the process, particularly in matters dealing with the executive, legislative and judiciary systems, including the protection of human rights and the freedom of the media, of religion, of minority peoples and languages and of political prisoners.

Since accession, all election-related issues have proven to be the defining issues in relations between Azerbaijan and the CoE. Azerbaijan undertook an obligation to adopt a unified election code at least six months prior to the next election (the October 2003 presidential elections). In 2002, under pressure from the Council of Europe, the Office of the President finally started work on a draft of the code, which would serve as a unified document for the country's entire electoral system and would aim to eradicate contradictions and gaps among various laws related to elections.

The New Election Law: A Key Domestic Issue
For these reasons, in 2002–2003, the process of elaborating a new electoral law became a major domestic political topic. This project was ascribed great importance by all parties because it would establish the ground rules for the presidential elections in 2003 and the crucial parliamentary elections in 2005. From the viewpoint of the international community (specifically, the OSCE and the CoE), the aim of this electoral-law project was to create a foundation which would allow the next elections to meet democratic standards and en-

sure that the election results were accepted by the majority of the participants.[4]

The new election code was designed to comply with international standards and the recommendations issued by the OSCE/Office for Democratic Institutions and Human Rights (ODIHR) based on its experience in international election monitoring. Experts from ODIHR and the Venice Commission of the Council of Europe have, since the summer of 2002, been working closely with the Azerbaijani presidential administration responsible for the preparation of this law. The drafts by this administration are put under continuous review and are discussed at meetings of experts.

The intention of the new electoral law was also to accommodate the interests of the various political parties, enabling participants in the coming elections at least to agree on the ground rules, and create a minimal measure of reciprocal trust. Without this, democratic elections cannot be held, even with the best of electoral laws.

Internal Discussion

Round Table Meetings
A public consultation process was deemed necessary to complement the expert meetings. While it is the sovereign right of a state to reform its election system, fundamental legislative changes should be based on a broad political consensus, in order to ensure the widest public confidence in the reform process and its outcome. As an initial step, in October 2002, the director of the OSCE/ODIHR arranged for a round table meeting to be conducted with President Heidar Aliev in December of that year. Other round table meetings were planned for early 2003.

The initial round table meeting, held on 17 and 18 December 2002 was, however, only a limited success, owing to the boycott by important opposition parties. These parties demanded that formal negotiations be held instead, and that the results of such negotiations should be binding, with the appoint-

---

4   Ambassador Peter Burkhard, Head of the OSCE Office in Baku, interview in *Yeni Musavat* newspaper, 16 November 2002. Also Opinion No. 222 (2000) *Azerbaijan's application for membership of the Council of Europe* (http://assembly.CE.int/main. asp?Link=/documents/adoptedtext/ta00/eopi222.htm).

ment of an arbitration commission. All the same, this event was the reason why the draft law, which had hitherto been confidential, was made public in late November. This led to intensive discussions within interested circles of NGOs and opposition parties. Within the latter group, a comprehensive commentary was elaborated, with detailed opinions on specific provisions of the draft law. The central focus during these discussions was on the election commission, a theme that dominated to the exclusion of virtually all other topics.[5]

Following the round table meeting, international organisations working in Baku concentrated on encouraging the leading members of the major political parties to reconcile their interests, with the aim of incorporating the results of this into the draft law. After some apparent initial successes involving agreements on format and procedures, the undertaking experienced a setback, when the opposition parties laid down new conditions which proved irreconcilable with the agreed principles. The enterprise failed completely when the party representatives invited to a meeting to resolve the situation did not show up, although they had originally agreed to attend.

Limited Exchange of Ideas
In March 2003, with some seven months left until the next elections, the international community managed to arrange for the senior civil servant in charge of the draft law (within the Office of the President), who is also the author of the law, to meet with the opposition's leading election expert, for an initial exchange of ideas on some of its central points. This became possible after the opposition's election experts said they would agree to a meeting of

---

5   Elections in Azerbaijan are administered by a three-tiered system of election commissions, headed by the 15-member Central Election Commission. There are 125 constituency election commissions and 5,137 polling station election commissions. The commissions play a crucial role in the conduct of elections, and their impartiality is of a paramount importance for the conduct of free and fair elections. Since Azerbaijan's independence, the composition of the election commissions always favoured the incumbent authorities and undermined confidence in the independence of the election administration; pro-government parties have a majority in all election commissions, sufficient to make all decisions. Moreover, the chairpersons of all election commissions are nominated by the parliamentary majority.

this kind, in order to discuss the provisions of the draft law, without prioritising any specific issues.

At this first meeting, both sides agreed on a roadmap for further discussions on the draft law. However, only one other meeting was held. This was due to the fact that the opposition expert's mandate was restricted, by the opposition parties, to what was considered to be the most crucial aspect of electoral reform: the establishment of the election commission. On hearing this, the government representative declared that, under these changed conditions, further discussion would be pointless.

Proposing International Organisation Involvement

The last hope of fulfilling, by way of an agreement between key political forces, the criterion set by the ODIHR and Council of Europe experts – that the election commission, and thus the electoral process, not be under the influence or control of a single political power – seemed to be in jeopardy. The international experts made it clear that neither the government's draft nor the opposition's counterproposal was acceptable from this point of view. Within the international community in Baku, opinion was growing that the international experts should draft a proposal themselves, which could then be developed further by experts working jointly from the ODIHR and the CoE. This proposal was subsequently accepted by the government and then forwarded to the appropriate parliamentary committee.

The Draft Law

In the meantime, the legislature had held a first reading and debate of the draft law. In the debate on the second reading, on 7 May 2003, members of the governing party were highly critical of the proposed changes and the international organisations involved. The draft was sent back to the committee for further discussion, which presented the changes to the plenum in a modified form. On 27 May 2003, this version was finally adopted by parliament. At the time, the view was that the new Code appeared to meet international standards in most respects, but that further amendment was required in order to meet some substantial shortcomings.[6]

---

6   Joint Final Assessment of the Electoral Code of the Republic of Azerbaijan, by OSCE/ODIHR and the European Commission for Democracy Through Law. Venice Commission, Council of Europe. http://venice.CE.int/docs/2003/CDL(2003)054-e.asp

3. Domestic Election Observers and Current Law: Notable Changes

Initial Observations

A Generally Satisfactory Outcome
The rules and practices concerning election observation are crucial for the success of elections, particularly if, as in the case of Azerbaijan, the question of election commissions has not been solved on a consensual basis. The international experts assessing the Code concluded in their final statement that 'the rules concerning election observation are generally satisfactory.' The rules over who may act as a domestic observer are set out in the text and appear to be broad (articles 40.6–40.7). The Code clearly stipulates the wide-ranging rights of candidates, party agents and their representatives, together with journalists and observers, to attend electoral commission meetings, access election documents, obtain copies of decisions, and observe the voting and counting process (Article 40). They are also allowed to observe the work of election commissions on Election Day and to include their observations in the commissions' protocols. They can also observe the transfer of election documents from the constituency election commissions to the CEC. The Code also foresees the right of NGOs to accredit observers (article 40.5).

A Notable Limitation
Despite this, until October 2005, public associations, including those receiving foreign state funding, were prevented from observing the electoral process. This prohibition was not a part of the electoral code itself, but of the 'Law on Public Unions and Foundations'. This law, passed in 2000, gave only local NGOs that received less than 30% of their funding from foreign entities the right to monitor elections. In practice, this disqualified an overwhelming majority of Azerbaijani NGOs, given the low levels of domestic funding available to them. This legal provision seriously impeded the work of local election observation up to 2005, as NGOs were unable to mobilise larger observation groups, train them and co-ordinate their activities. Indirectly, this provision also made individual observers more susceptible to intimidation, since they

lacked the protection of a larger organisation. This law also affected the financial transparency of the NGOs, since it discouraged them from disclosing the money which they had received from international donors (in order to preserve their ability to field observer teams). Since the introduction of the Election Code, right up until the recent parliamentary elections, local NGOs mitigated the impact of this restriction by registering their members as individual monitors, a right granted under the Law.

Legal Alterations

The international community, as well as domestic NGOs, repeatedly voiced serious concerns over this shortcoming, as it breaches relevant provisions of the 1990 OSCE Copenhagen Document, relating to civil organisations. In their final assessment of the Election Code, the OSCE/ODIHR and Venice Commission of the CoE stated: 'despite the fact that the prohibition of foreign funding of local NGOs does not seem to violate the Constitution of Azerbaijan, the objections against such a rule stem from the opinion that comprehensive observation by domestic and international observers promotes transparency and increases public confidence in the electoral process.' [7]

This discriminatory provision was abolished in 2005, only two weeks prior to the 6 November parliamentary elections. On 25 October, President Aliev issued an executive order that called on the parliament and the Central Election Commission to introduce a series of measures that would help to prevent multiple voting, remove restrictions on election observers, establish complaints procedures, and enhance accountability for electoral violations.

Work In Progress?

On 28 October, in response to this presidential order, the parliament lifted the ban that had prevented foreign-funded NGOs from acting as observers in the elections. However, the late introduction of the order made it impossible for domestic observation groups to benefit, as there was no time left to attract the

---

7   *Joint Final Assessment of the Electoral Code of the Republic of Azerbaijan,* by OSCE/ODIHR and the European Commission for Democracy Through Law. Venice Commission, Council of Europe. http://venice.CE.int/docs/2003/CDL(2003)054-e.asp

funds needed in order to organise a comprehensive domestic election observation effort. It will not be possible to assess the changes that this legal modification will bring to domestic observation groups until the by-elections scheduled for 13 May 2006.

4. NGOs and Current Law Practice

The Current Situation

Significant Hurdles
The government of Azerbaijan severely restricts the activities of NGOs. The right to the freedom of association is guaranteed by the Constitution of the Republic of Azerbaijan (from 1995). While the European Convention on Human Rights recognises the right of the people to form associations with no special requirements for formalisation (registration) of such association, domestic legislation – the Law of the Republic of Azerbaijan On the Registration of Legal Entities and State Register of Legal Entities – stipulates that non-governmental organisations must have state-registered status in order to operate. The Ministry of Justice is authorised as the state agency tasked with registering public associations.

In Azerbaijan, NGOs are poorly recognised by governmental officials. As a result, most of them have difficulties in obtaining the required registration status with the Ministry of Justice. In the past three to four years, hundreds of NGO applications for registration, lodged with the Ministry, have either remained unanswered, or have been rejected. The lack of registered status significantly restricts NGOs from functioning properly, and also restricts donors from providing unregistered NGOs with financial support. While Azerbaijani legislation establishes clear and exhaustive requirements for setting up a public organisation, officials of the Ministry of Justice usually reject the registration of NGOs on groundless basis, or through misinterpretation of the laws.[8]

Growing Activity
All the same, NGOs in Azerbaijan are very active in organising non-partisan election observation and voter education activities. With every new election,

---

8   *Report on the registration procedure of NGOs in Azerbaijan*, OSCE Office in Baku at: http://www.osce.org/documents/ob/2005/05/14151_en.pdf Problems of NGO registration in Azerbaijan at: http://www.osce.org/documents/ob/2003/08/558_en.pdf

the organisational, observation capacity and professional skills of these domestic groups have been growing.

The presidential elections in 2003 substantially increased the level of NGO
activity in the political sphere. Despite numerous complaints about the difficulties associated with registration, large numbers of domestic observers, from
political parties and NGOs as well as individuals, were accredited. On Election Day, over 40,000 domestic observers were deployed around the country.

Several groups united under the umbrella agency, 'For the Sake of Fair
Elections', and organised a unified election-monitoring campaign throughout
the country. Also the Election Monitoring Centre, made up of 12 NGOs, conducted election monitoring. Additionally, it produced campaign-oriented television programmes aimed at educating voters on voter registration and encouraging election participation. The Women's Rights Protection Centre conducted training of observers in several regions. Another alliance of NGOs,
'SOS-03', also conducted various activities aimed at increasing voter turnout.

Historical Problems

Recurrent Issues
During the 2004 municipal elections, domestic NGOs also managed to deploy
thousands of observers, despite the existing legal restrictions. In 2005, several NGOs, including the Election Monitoring Centre, For the Sake of Civil
Society, and the Co-ordinating Advisory Council for Free and Fair Elections,
deployed large numbers of short-term observers on Election Day. However,
assessing the activities of these groups, it seems clear that NGOs involved in
election observation in Azerbaijan have, over the years, faced the same kinds
of problems. These are presented below.

Local executive authorities and police often interfere with the activities of
the observers before, during and after Election Day. In rural areas, observers
who witness violations such as ballot stuffing are pressured by the representatives of the local executives not to report them.

Very often observers are denied access to polling stations, or are expelled
from them. Observers are required to sit far away from voting or counting and
thus are prevented from observing these processes effectively. Furthermore,
they are unable to collect tabulation protocols.

Most importantly, no effective sanctions are imposed on representatives of local executive authorities who, in violation of the law, have interfered in the election process. This diminishes confidence in the rule of law and opens the way for further violations.

All these problems result from:

- first and foremost, the lack of political will, on behalf of the Azerbaijani authorities, to hold free and fair elections
- the composition of election commissions, which favours those currently in office (in many cases, election commissions act together with the representatives of local authorities in violating the rights of domestic observers)
- the inability of most observation groups to act in an impartial, unbiased and professional manner
- arbitrary application of the Election Law and almost total impunity of those responsible for violations of the Law
- lack of knowledge on the provisions of the Election Code among commission members
- lack of understanding and knowledge, on the part of observers, of their rights, duties and responsibilities.

Puppet NGOs

The work of NGOs in the electoral process is further complicated by the fact that political groups have established 'puppet NGOs' to promote their own agendas. The existence of such groups, which claim the same status as non-partisan NGOs, makes it difficult for NGOs to mount election observation efforts which the people can trust, and tarnishes their accomplishments.

Internal Bickering
Another challenging internal obstacle that faces most NGOs is their inability to articulate a clear message and work together to promote that message. They tend to criticise government plans rather than formulate independent so-

lutions to the problems facing Azerbaijan, and they lack crucial skills like coalition-building. Too often, their messages are driven by the personal interests of strong personalities, which can in turn contribute to fragmentation of the mission.

Lack of Public Support

The most significant obstacle to the activities of NGOs in Azerbaijan is the lack of public trust and popular support. Recent polls (SRC, Public Opinion Survey, 'Lessons learned from the Parliamentary Elections', 2005) show that the vast majority of the population (87%) does not believe that reports or recommendations submitted shortly after the election make any difference. Usually, these reports are reported only summarily in the media, at home and abroad. Occasionally the government acts on some of the less important observations and recommendations. More serious recommendations, i.e. those that could truly improve the overall situation of the conduct of the elections, are usually put aside, as there is no established practice for officials to take note of such reports and recommendations. There are the rare cases where the reports of Election Observation Missions have made a dramatic difference, such as in Ukraine or in Georgia – but those are the exceptions. The more general rule, especially in Azerbaijan, is that the reports are simply shelved, thus diminishing the impact of the observation efforts of domestic and international groups.

5. Election Observation in Azerbaijan: What More Could Be Done?

First Suggestion: Further Legislative Changes

There are still some gaps in domestic election legislation that need to be addressed. For instance, the Election Code should specify that observers have a role, and a right of access, in electoral commissions, starting after polling day and continuing until all the electoral tasks are completed. This would increase the transparency of the activities of the commissions, especially the CEC, in the crucial days before the announcement of the final results. The Election Code should also be amended to provide for a simple procedure (at PEC level) for the registration of individual observers.

Second Suggestion: Improvements within Domestic Observation Groups

Focusing on a Long-Term Study

The integrity and success of the observation process depends upon the professionalism and independence of the observer missions. Domestic groups should pay more attention to the training of personnel to be deployed at polling stations on Election Day. They should also avoid the practice of drawing conclusions only from observations made on Election Day itself, and should instead focus on long-term observation efforts, not least on what happens after the elections are over.

Raising Public Awareness

Domestic observation groups should also actively promote their work through the media and raise public awareness on the importance of their activities. It is essential that the domestic groups make every effort possible to ensure that they conduct their activities in an impartial manner. Local NGOs should restore the confidence of the public by concise, factual and independent reporting of what has been observed.

Domestic groups should look into ways of encouraging greater public attention to the reports of Election Observer Missions, and find a way to increase public participation in encouraging the authorities to act on the recommendations of an observation mission. Independent NGOs involved in election observation should try to establish coalitions, so as to be able to work as efficiently and cost-effectively as possible.

6. Conclusions

At the end of the day, will all this help? If the process of improving the Electoral Code continues in Azerbaijan, will the new amendments introduced to the Election Law make any change in practice? Will the change in tactics applied in the work of domestic observation groups lead to positive developments?

It is true that the sovereign governments are under no effective obligation to act on recommendations by domestic or even international observers. There are many examples where Azerbaijani authorities have implemented several minor or technical recommendations for electoral reform, but held back on the most important suggestions. There are also examples where laws have been changed by the legislature, but not implemented in practice: this creates an illusion of reform, but no real change. In reality, in Azerbaijan, it is the scrupulous implementation of both the spirit and the letter of the law that will serve as a key test of the political will to conduct democratic elections. It is possible to have an imperfect election law, and yet have elections that are fair and free – and visa versa.

The country's 'democratic development' is one of the main commitments Azerbaijan made to the OSCE and to the Council of Europe. Azerbaijani officials often talk about 'stability and development'. It is clear what they mean by 'stability', but it is more difficult to grasp what they mean by 'development'. If all they are talking about is economic development, then this is too narrow a definition – and, additionally, it is a mistaken one.

The key issues are these: to what extent does the will of the people form the basis of power and how much is it taken into account in decision-making? To what extent does the existing situation allow the votes whose opinion differs from that of the majority make an impact on the political processes?

If the development of Azerbaijan is to be sustainable, it will have to promote the implementation of a fundamental democratic principle: that political decisions and laws should be prepared and enacted by means of a transparent process which takes account of the broadest possible spectrum of interests. The leaders of the country (not only those in power, but also in the opposition) must always be committed to the democratic process and the building of democratic institutions, and respect human rights in all aspects. Civil society must be increasingly involved, and a firm commitment to democratic reforms should be in place. The promotion of these principles, as well as greater transparency and participation, will be of decisive importance in ensuring the sustainability of Azerbaijan's transformation into a genuinely democratic state.

III PARLIAMENTARY ELECTIONS IN AZERBAIJAN: DEMOCRATIC EXPECTATIONS VERSUS IMITATED REALITIES

Zafar Guliev

1. Introduction

Promising Conditions

On the eve of the 2005 Azerbaijani parliamentary elections, there were certain grounds for careful optimism. These grounds had been created by the direction in which the development of certain political processes in the world was taking, both in the post-Soviet area and in Azerbaijani society. The situation helped to re-animate the faith in the possibility of an evolutionary, or revolutionary, advancement of the country towards democracy.

Inaugural Address of President Bush
In his January 2005 inaugural address, US President G.W. Bush declared that support for democracy would henceforth be the main priority. Furthermore, US foreign policy, as well as the official line from Washington, would always be side by side with those who were fighting for freedom. Former US policy towards developing countries had been founded on the formula of 'first stability, then democracy'. However, several months after the Bush inaugural speech, the US Secretary of State, Condoleezza Rice, specified a 'new course' for the White House. She publicly announced that the former US policy was erroneous and that, from then on, the Bush Administration would support stability only on the basis of democracy.

Further Confirmation

In the spring of 2005, while speaking in public in Tbilisi, the US President once again confirmed the priority and importance of democracy in this 'new course', and declared an intention to actively support the struggle for freedom of the people of the Southern Caucasus. At the start of the parliamentary election campaign in Azerbaijan, several influential US political figures (among them Madeleine Albright, Paul Dobriansky and Senator Richard Lugar) made a series of visits to Baku. During these visits, they sought to convince the Azerbaijani public that there were no alternatives to democratic elections, nor could there even be any *possibility* of such alternatives. In his frequent travels around the country, Rino Harnish, US Ambassador to Azerbaijan, tried to re-animate the public's trust in the West and in democracy, as this had been strained by the scandalous presidential elections of 2003. During the election campaign, all the Western emissaries actively demonstrated the seriousness of their democratic intentions. They were unequivocal about the importance of the situation: either there would be fair elections, or there would be an 'orange revolution'. Finally, at a press conference in Baku two weeks prior to the elections, Daniel Fried, Assistant Secretary of State, made an open declaration on behalf of the entire US administration: this time, Washington would adhere to the principle to the end, and would not sacrifice democracy for its own personal oil interests in Azerbaijan.

The Turning Tide

If the West (especially the USA) had in fact remained faithful to this position to the end, then the ruling regime would hardly have been able to succeed at falsifying the results of the elections with such unceremonious ease. More importantly, they would not have been able to legitimise such a scandalous victory once again. If the undemocratic and falsified steps of the Aliev regime had run up against the co-ordinated, rigid and principled position of democratic forces, both inside the country and abroad, this could have led to a different development of the election and post-election situation. But alas!

The 2005 Azerbaijani parliamentary elections were held in much the same way as before: under extremely undemocratic conditions and under the habitual 'total falsification' regime. Within the context of the inauguration promises of G.W. Bush, and taking into account the unparalleled attention given to the election process by international organisations, a rightful, more equitable and more adequate response by the West would have been to acknowledge the scale of election fraud, as well as the open sabotage of democracy norms by the ruling Azerbaijan regime.

Despite the moderate nature and reserve of their assessments, in their preliminary report, OSCE observers nevertheless had to recognise the fact of the undemocratic nature of the elections, and the lack of consistency with international standards. Europe's position proved more adequate and principled, whereas the White House administration once again sacrificed democracy for the sake of geopolitical, oil and other pragmatic interests. Initially the USA, in a reserved manner, supported the OSCE. Later, however, it reverted to hypocrisy, announcing a *plat du jour* formula, about 'following the path of Azerbaijan towards democracy'.

Other Relevant Limitations

Of course, the possibilities of the world democratic community are not unlimited. At this present time, the structures of the Council of Europe and the USA do not possess sufficiently reliable legal levers to enable a direct, preventive impact on an authoritarian regime, i.e. one which could force such a regime into observing the norms of elective democracy. Nor do they have at their disposal effective, peaceful sanctions against regimes that demonstratively violate democratic requirements and intentionally sabotage the recommendations of the West. But what the issue involves is not so much the range of possibilities and the effectiveness of sanctions, as the consistency, adequacy, and level of principle of the Western position. For a significant section of the Azerbaijani public, it was important that the post-election assessments made by the West should not deviate from earlier democratic assertions; Europe and the USA should remain principled to the end, and not allow geopolitical, oil and other pragmatic interests triumph over the interests of freedom and human rights. The Azerbaijani public were right to expect an adequate response from Europe and the USA regarding the demonstrative sabotage of democratic norms during the parliamentary elections. Had the West recurrently participated in the Aliev regime's game of imitating democracy, this would have had extremely negative consequences for the development of all political processes in Azerbaijan.

2. The Election Environment

The Azerbaijani parliamentary elections held on 6 November were the third set of elections since the country had acquired independence. The first two election experiences (for the legislative body of the country in 1995 and 2000), had occurred during the reign of Heidar Aliev, a politician shaped in the bosom of the totalitarian Soviet practice, and well-versed in imitation, including the imitation of the election process. Both experiences proved to be far not only from international standards, but also from basic requirements of common sense. These initial elections were held under a regime of total falsification, typical of the formation of parliaments during Soviet times, based on the system of using 'rosters'. The 2005 elections were not to be an exception, even though they were held under somewhat different political conditions, with the enhanced pressure of the international community and against the backdrop of the growth of revolutionary expectations in society. Furthermore, society was under the 'patronage' of the formally new (neo-monarchist) system of power in the country. Despite these innovations, and contrary to the expectations of many, the election process from the beginning to the end followed the time-tested Aliev regime scheme of imitation. Once again, it ended with the formation of the legislative body of the country on the basis of the 'roster'.

Previous Parliamentary Elections

In order to determine the statistical characteristics of the most recent elections, and take into account the new factors, it is appropriate to compare briefly the current situation with the previous parliamentary elections.

The 1995 Parliamentary Elections
These were conducted on the basis of a mixed system of 100 majority mandates and 24 proportional mandates. Out of twelve parties that submitted documents, only eight were allowed to take part in the elections based on the proportional system. The camp of the democratic opposition was represented by two parties, Popular Front and National Independence, whereas Musavat

and other opposition parties were not allowed to take part. A total of 1,040 candidates tried to compete for the 100 majority mandates, but the Central Election Commission (CEC) allowed only 387 to participate in the elections. Of this number, only 10% were candidates from the opposition parties, while the rest, including those formally labelled 'non-party candidates', were in fact representatives and allies of the ruling power. All the election commissions were under the monopolistic control of the ruling party. The results of the elections were totally falsified. The parliament was in fact 'elected' on the basis of rosters drawn up in the Office of the President. The aggregate of the opposition received only ten mandates. The West contented itself with reserved criticism, and assessed the elections as a step forward on the way to democracy.

The Parliamentary Elections of 2000
These took place under the same mixed system of majority and proportional mandates. More than 20 parties attempted to participate in the elections, but only 13 managed to submit rosters with signatures to the CEC in time. The CEC initially allowed only five parties into the elections (again having excluded Musavat, the liberal and the democratic parties). Later, on the insistence of the USA and the Council of Europe, all 13 parties joined in the struggle for the votes of the electorate. In all, 1,040 majority candidates competed for the 100 majority mandates, but the CEC allowed only 409 to take part in the elections. As in 1995, most of the majority candidates (formally 'non-party' as well as party candidates) were representatives and adherents of the ruling power: around 320 out of 407. The election commissions, under CoE pressure, were initially formed on a pseudo-parity basis (1/3 from the ruling party, 1/3 from the parliamentary opposition and 1/3 from a bloc of the allegedly independent deputies). However, not long before the elections, they were revised in a manner that meant an even greater strengthening of the positions of the ruling power. Once again, the elections were held under the regime of total falsification, based on the rosters drawn up by the ruling power. The scale of the fraud, and the international resonance as a result of this, forced those in power to turn to additional methods of imitation: in 11 territorial election committees, the results of the voting were annulled; new elections were scheduled – which were then held in the same fraudulent manner. The de-

mocratic opposition (who actually won a widespread victory in the elections, but ended up receiving a mere 15 mandates) mutually agreed not to recognise the results of the voting. Part of the opposition (Musavat, National Independence and PNFA) remained true to this decision and rejected the mandates, while the other part (the Popular Front and The Civil Solidarity Parties) reneged, and joined in with the work of the parliament. As the result, the democratic opposition camp in the parliament was once again represented by ten deputies. And once again, the West limited itself to a *plat du jour* criticism, addressed to the ruling power of Azerbaijan, and pronounced the elections to be the next step on the way towards democracy. It was on the basis of the results of these elections that Azerbaijan was accepted as a member of the Council of Europe in January 2001.

The 2005 Parliamentary Elections
For the first time, elections were held based purely on a majority system, in 125 single-mandate territorial election commissions. The CEC registered practically all candidates, and the final figure was record-high: over 2,060 competitors (although this was reduced to 1,544 by the time of the elections, due to voluntary or forced rejection of candidates' nominations, or disqualification by the courts). The main political force went to the elections with single rosters: this included the ruling party 'New Azerbaijan' (*Jeny Azerbaijan*) and the leading opposition bloc 'Азадлыг' ('Azadlyg', including Musavat, the New Front and the democratic parties). A total of over 430 candidates competed on behalf of the ruling party. Altogether, around two thirds of the registered candidates were open or discreet adherents of the ruling elite. The remaining third part were, in approximately equal proportion, representatives of the opposition and of independent competitors.

All election commissions were headed by representatives of the ruling party (who also clearly predominated in the commissions in terms of numbers of members). During these elections, finger marking and exit polls were used for the first time. During the elections, 1,586 international and 57,000 local observers were involved. Once again, however, the elections were held under extremely undemocratic conditions and the results were totally falsified – indeed, evidence of this was provided by the OSCE reports and the reports of many influential international organisations. Under pressure from the West, and within the framework of their own election-imitation scenario, the ruling powers annulled the results of the elections in ten constituencies and called new elections. In addition, the results of voting in two constituencies were corrected. According to public opinion polls and the assessments of many experts, the democratic opposition had in fact won at least half of the seats in parliament. Based on even the distorted data of the exit polls (due to the atmosphere of total falsification), the democratic opposition was to get around 30% of the seats in parliament (some 40 mandates).Alongside this, the official results of the elections (without taking the ten constituencies into account) were as follows: 56 mandates to the ruling party; 5 to pro-governmental parties; 6 to representatives of moderate or 'pocket' opposition; and 41 to the so-called 'independent' candidates, who were in reality active allies of those in power. The genuine opposition received a paltry seven mandates in the parliament – fewer than in the previous elections. The united forces of the opposition, and those sympathising with them, represented over 500 candidates. They refused to recognise the results of the elections and held a series of peaceful protest actions involving many thousands of people. The last of these peaceful actions, on 26 November, was brutally suppressed by police forces. After the Constitutional Court had approved the elections, the opposition declined the option of participating in the re-elections in the ten constituencies, and rejected the chance to be involved in the work of the illegitimate parliament. Thus, the new parliament is unlikely to have any representation of the real opposition. Preliminary Western assessments of the election results were ambivalent. The European structures recognised that the elections did not match international standards, and at the January Session of PACE they threatened the Azerbaijani government with sanctions. The USA had previously held the European position, but now hurriedly announced its recognition of the new Azerbaijani parliament, in which real opposition would not be represented. Once again, Washington's position made a mockery of the words 'the next step on the way towards democracy'.

3. Imitating Democracy

The current election process took place in an atmosphere that felt the firm pressure of international organisations. Additionally, in the background, were the increased revolutionary expectations in society. Furthermore, there were various undoubted innovations (finger marking, exit poll, an unprecedented number of candidates and observers, etc). All the same, the attitude towards the elections, and the model of behaviour of the ruling regime, did not change in the least. The imitation strategy, repeatedly and successfully tested by Heidar Aliev, was realised in its full scope by Ilham Aliev, who followed on from Geidov's deeds, during the most recent election campaign. Let us see how this unsophisticated strategy works:

Creating a Good First Impression

Long before the start of the election campaign, the President and his team agree to almost all the wishes of the West, and give assurances that they will create the necessary conditions for holding open and fair elections. In the early stages, the ruling regime does not question its obligations toward observing general democracy standards. For some time, the ruling power puts aside its standard arguments – that the elections are 'our internal business', that the West is not our commander, and that 'other (methods of) democracy' corresponds more to our mentality, etc. At this initial stage, Ilham Aliev publicly demonstrates, towards the world community, a clear predisposition towards 'Western democracy' (as his father had done in former years), showing that he is fully prepared to project this onto the Azerbaijani elections. His methods of democratic imitation are indicative: the 'prisoners of October' are released; amnesty granted to many political prisoners; the protracted moratorium on meetings is withdrawn; and additionally his decree of 11 May promises fair and equitable elections.

Dropping the Mask

However, as soon as the official discussion phase of the election legislation and the final formulation of the legal elections basis begin (in the parliament), the behaviour of the ruling powers changes. At this point, the President retreats into the shadows and arrangements for his scenario are implemented, publicly and actively, by a team consisting of the president's office, the ruling party, and the administration of the parliament. At this second (legal) stage, it is as if the ruling powers suffer from amnesia; they forget about all their democratic promises and even become somewhat aggressive towards the West. The propaganda of other theses are utilised instead: the sovereignty of the country and its independence from the dictatorship of the West, the specific mentality of the people, their specific attitude towards democracy, etc. If, in the first stage, all these arguments were intentionally put aside, then in the second stage they become the basis for 'legalising' the elections, providing the enemy with the widest opportunities of falsifying the results. At the very last moment, the President enters the stage and appeals to 'our values' (independence, mentality, the people, etc) and the requirements of the public. He then approves the decision of the 'sovereign' parliament and begins the election campaign.

Propaganda

During the third phase, the election campaign, the President once again withdraws, while the ruling regime openly demonstrates reactionary behaviour, ignoring even its own legal base of the elections. At this decisive stage, the ruling regime makes active use of its administrative and financial resources, its propagandistic information, as well as its 'black PR' and outspoken repressions against the opposition. This creates the necessary basis for successful falsification of the election results. As a rule, at the final stage of this phase, prolonged and behind-the scenes bargaining takes place among the main participants in the election process (the West, the ruling power and, in part, the opposition). The West, whose expectations have been deceived, publicly demonstrates its irritation with the uncompromising and undemocratic behaviour of the ruling power. Furthermore, it is insistent in its recommendation that at least some legal and procedural amendments should be introduced into the election process. The opposition, vexed at this course of events, expresses its disappointment and anger with threats of meetings, revolution, and election boycott. At this point, the ruling power, having scared everyone with its reactionary behaviour, deliberately delays the bargaining and desperately defends the conquered legal thresholds, while trying to 'pay (it all) off' with small concessions. Negotiations are generally concluded in the following manner: on the day before the elections, the ruling power, in a particularly democracy-imitative manner, agrees to some of the recommendations of the West, slightly lessening its reactionary pressure on the opposition – all the while managing to maintain general control over the election process. This takes place in the form of giving the appearance of being 'the saviour of the people'. This means that, once again, the President enters centre stage, utters beautiful words, reprimands a handful of officials, calms down the world and the domestic community, and uses methods of imitation (for instance, his directives at the operational meeting on 25 October gave the promise of fair elections). This phase is always concluded in the same way, by the total falsification of the voters' will, and the formation of the legislative body of the country based on the roster. Heidar Aliev acted in the same manner during the parliamentary elections in 1995 and in 2000.

Election Falsification

Then, during the last, post-election stage, the aim of legitimising the fraudulent elections begins. Once again, the President comes onstage, anticipating the official results, declares that the elections were generally fair, and that the party he heads deserves to win the victory... adding that, of course, there were some occasional violations, which will immediately be dealt with and the guilty punished. Next, within the framework of the imitation scenario, and working in co-ordination with the Office of the President, the CEC annuls the results of the elections in several constituencies – as a rule, those where the representatives of the opposition happened to have won. The prosecutor's office finds several scapegoats, while the Constitutional Court approves the results of the elections in such form as initially envisaged by the authorities.

At this stage, the ruling powers brutally quash all protest actions, trying with all means at their disposal to force the opposition and society to resign themselves to the 'results' of the elections. In respect of the West, those in power demonstrate the behaviour that was characteristic of the initial stage of the election campaign: patiently listening to criticism, recognising certain weaknesses, promising to improve in the future and to take all the wishes into account. The West, as a rule, is satisfied with these imitation methods and with the words 'the Aliev regime', and practically wraps up its active mission on democratisation in Azerbaijan, until the next elections are due. This then is the schematic model of imitation of all elections in Azerbaijan.

4. 2005: Parallels with Previous Elections

Parallels with the previous parliamentary elections are also seen in the context of the model of the reactionary actions of the ruling regime: the same repressive methods, based on propaganda. In the course of the election campaign the customary scenario of the 'threat of a coup d'etat' is brought up; a
nationwide defamation campaign against the opposition starts; measures are
undertaken to heighten police preparedness. There are mass arrests, as well
as searches, court hearings, cleansing, and so on.

The 1995 Parliamentary Elections

The situation was the same in 1995. The ruling power discovered a series of
'plots' and thus withdrew several parties from the contest (the Musavat, Islamic, Labour and Communist Parties); held a show trial involving journalists
from the satirical newspaper *Cheshme*; organised a series of searches of
mass media editorial offices; arrested some prominent politicians; and actively carried out a propaganda campaign of 'witch hunting'.

The 2000 Parliamentary Elections

A similar scenario was repeated in the parliamentary elections of 2000. In
August, the head of the Julfinsky branch of the Musavat Party was arrested,
accused of hijacking a passenger plane. Several days later, the chief editor of
the popular opposition newspaper *Jeny Musavat,* Rauf Arifogly, was arrested
as well. Those arrested, as well as the Musavat Party and the entire democratic community were accused of involvement in developing a political act of
terrorism, and in plans to destabilise the situation and overthrow the ruling
power. The apparatus of the ruling power immediately turned its propaganda
machine up into full capacity. It attempted a long shot – to divert attention
from elections, to label Musavata a terrorist organisation, and to gain the tacit
approval of the West and the public so that it could adopt strict measures
against the opposition. Immediately after the elections, the ruling powers bru-

tally suppressed the social disturbances in Shecky, having identified them as an attempt by the opposition to stage a coup d'etat.

The Recent Parliamentary Elections

The ruling power went even further in the recent elections. Initially, a special operation was carried out against Ruslan Bashiri, the leader of a youth organisation. It was presented as though the youth organisation had been preparing a coup d'etat, and then accompanied this with an unruly campaign around the 'national persecution' of the opposition (focusing primarily on the persecution of People's Front and its leader). Later on, a political show was staged around the return of ex-Speaker Rasul Guliev: this was skilfully transformed into the 'disclosure' of yet another coup d'etat, allegedly planned by some powerful domestic oligarchs together with the opposition. This repressive propagandist show, marked by mass dismissals and arrests on behalf of the ruling party, was stopped for some time. But it could have been revived again at any moment, had either of the following situations occurred: there was a need to eliminate disagreeable persons in the ruling team, or there was a need to threaten and punish the democratic opposition if it could not be tamed to accept the results of the elections.

No significant innovations (that is, positive innovations) could be observed in the election strategy or the model of behaviour of the Aliev regime. The same practice of imitation, the same reactionary attitude, the same falsification and undemocratic tricks, and the same methods of controlling of the election campaign were practised. And it is not clear on what basis the Western politicians placed their careful optimism as to the possibility of an evolutionary self-renewal of the Aliev regime. Is it, indeed, the sad experience of all previous years, with insufficient confirmation of the Aliev regime's right to rule? Or are the new falsifications necessary, in order to finish off society's confidence in democracy for once and for all?

5. Examining the New Optimism

On the eve of the parliamentary elections, there was a certain basis for cautious optimism. But this was in no way connected with the possibility of the current system of power undergoing democratic self-improvement, nor was it pre-conditioned by the 'good will' and the head of the state's instructions of imitation. And it did not result from the development of the Aliev scenario within the election situation. The basis of this optimism was something different. The external and internal political background of the current elections had changed: indeed, the direction of the processes of development in the world had changed. Along with this, the priorities of many of the main participants in the post-Soviet space had also, to a certain extent, changed in terms of their positions, intentions and priorities – this includes the West, the opposition, or the electorate.

Attitudes

Pre-Election Position of the West
As elections approached, the West actively demonstrated an objective interest in qualitative change, in the liberalisation of the system of power in Azerbaijan, and in the continuation of the democratic rebuilding in the post-Soviet realm that had begun with Georgia and Ukraine. Both the USA and the CoE declared that they had revised some of their former priorities, and openly tried to brainwash the public of Azerbaijan into believing that they no longer intended to sacrifice democracy in the name of geopolitics, stability, and oil interests. If the West (especially the USA) had remained faithful to this position to the end, then this time it would have been difficult for the ruling regime to implement their scenario of total election falsification and, moreover, win and then approve, this scandalous victory. If the undemocratic and fraudulent steps of the Aliev regime had continuously encountered a co-ordinated, stern and principled response of the West, this could have acted as a catalyst for other, more encouraging and more promising variants of both the election and post-election development in Azerbaijan.

Inspiring Examples

Inspired by the verbal support of the West, and the success of the democratic forces in Georgia and Ukraine, the democratic opposition (initially, the bloc 'Azadlyg') focused on achieving a victory in the parliamentary elections. They were not going to content with getting a handful of mandates, because these would be based on the results of the ruling regime's falsified show, as they had been before. Throughout the election campaign, the opposition actively exaggerated its level of preparation for a 'velvet revolution' variant of the elections (i.e. with a democratic takeover). In a situation of total election fraud, the opposition intended to continue its struggle, counting on the support both inside the country and abroad. Given the scarcity of propagandists, as well as the limited financial, organisational and other resources of the opposition, then, if order to have any chances of success, this programme would need the active support of democracy from the West as well as from Azerbaijani society.

Passiveness of the Electorate

To a certain extent, the active pro-democratic rhetoric of the West, and the determination of the opposition, also revived the confidence of Azerbaijani society in the election process. However, this confidence did not manifest itself in active involvement in the political processes. The main mass of the electorate, although dissuaded by the viewpoints of the Aliev system, and craving quick democratic innovations, nevertheless steered clear of active participation in either the election or the post-election battles.

This passiveness on the part of society can be explained not so much by an indifference towards political issues, as by the presence of real doubts about the level of preparation, and ability, of the West and opposition to act firmly in favour of democracy. There was fear that the former post-election events would be repeated, whereby the ruling regime, having approved the falsified results of the elections, immediately started the prolonged process of 'creeping' in repressions, not only again the opposition itself, but also against those who had supported the opposition during the campaign. If the consistent and principled actions of the West and the opposition (on blocking the falsification or revolutionarily revising the unfair results of the elections) were undertaken at a high standard, and could inspire many citizens with confidence in the struggle for democracy, then the ruling regime, apparently, would have to target other members of society.

The Outcome

Unfortunately, the realities of the election process proved that even this cautious optimism was unfounded. The democratic opposition placed excessive reliance on the support of the West, and obediently followed its recommendations, frequently discarding both the requirements of the specific political situation at hand and the actual objectives of its active work with the electorate. In turn, the West had excessive hopes for the democratic promises of President Ilham Aliev, and was held captive by his myth of the possibility of a liberal transformation (or self-renovation) of power, the result of which would have to be cleaner and more open elections.

The West, actively pushing the Azerbaijani neo-monarchy along the path towards the evolutionary advancement of democracy, used the opposition, and the threat of the 'orange revolution', in the same manner as the ruling power – in order to exert pressure. In the end, the Western-initiated 'orange threat' (which many people sincerely believed in and were involved in together with the democratic opposition) proved to be simply a means of exerting pressure on those in power, to force them to undertake certain reform steps. In a sense, the West was trying to give the Azerbaijani rulers the following idea: either there would be an evolutionary movement towards democracy, or there would be a revolutionary compulsion towards it.

However, in response to all these admonitions and threats, the ruling regime, on the advice of influential Kremlin emissaries and political technologists, deliberately secured a plan of a preventive counter-revolution, and successfully implemented it during election process. As a result, neither the evolutionary hopes of the West nor the revolutionary expectations of the opposition came true. Under the disguise of a 'dangerous revolutionary scenario', the Aliev regime calmly falsified the results of the elections and formed a totally obedient parliament, as quickly as possible, while – as usual – ignoring the democratic expectations of its own people and of the international community.

6. The Post-Election Period

Constitutional Court Decision

On 2 December 2005, by a decision of the Constitutional Court, the parliamentary elections acquired legal status: 115 candidates received deputy mandates, while the destiny of 10 of the seats would be decided in re-elections, likely to be held without the participation of the real opposition. Thus ended an important stage in the post-Heidarian history of Azerbaijan; the neo-monarchic power elected (or, more accurately, appointed) the parliament in a manner that suited itself. Based on the results of the falsified elections, and obedient to the wishes of the president, a single-party parliament was formed, in which the real opposition of the country was not represented.

What this did was to doom the ruling regime to a confrontation with its own people and the international democratic community (this is already being observed), and also to a dangerous puppet dependence on the external forces of Moscow and Washington. Such a parliament cannot become a guarantor of long-term stability, nor can it be a catalyst for dynamic development in the country. It does not bring the promise of positive perspectives for society.

The USA and the CoE

The most unexpected surprise of the post-election period was the gradual degradation of the outwardly seamless and co-ordinated former position of the USA and the CoE as to the parliamentary elections in Azerbaijan. Currently a clear discrepancy between their pre- and post-election positions can be observed: the USA, which had initially encouraged the ruling regime with a 'stick', shifted to the position of encouraging it with 'carrots' alone. It appears as though the Council of Europe remains faithful to its democratic requirements, and demonstrates the threat of a 'stick in the form of sanctions'. If the attitudes of the USA and CoE towards the administration of Azerbaijan are the result of a spontaneous (as apposed to a co-ordinated) response to the election and post-election processes, then this creates good opportunities for the authorities of Azerbaijan to manoeuvre between America and Europe, and the possibility of continuing the drift towards Moscow.

What seems more likely is that is a case of carefully co-ordinated post-election behaviour of the USA and CoE, aimed at halting the escalation of anti-Western moods in Azerbaijani society, and preventing a pro-Kremlin drift on the part of official Baku (with the purpose of blocking the possibility of a 're-Sovietisation' and 'Uzbekistanisation' course for Azerbaijan). When we look at the situation in terms of this option, we can discern a well thought-out and co-ordinated policy in respect of Azerbaijan, whereby Europe 'works' with the opposition, while the USA works primarily with the ruling power, in hopes of preventing a situation where both groups retreat from the pro-Western and pro-democratic course. The co-ordinated 'stick and carrot' policy implemented by the USA and CoE can strengthen the promotion of a pro-US drift in Azerbaijan, while also keeping alive the hopes and options of the real opposition's struggle for democracy. By this, the USA and CoE hope that, through joint efforts and without serious sanctions, the country can revert to its former geopolitical course – a course that, despite well-tested democratic processes, will retain the leverage needed to maintain their impact on both the ruling power and opposition, as well as on the course of the development of events in Azerbaijan, keeping them firmly in the hands of the West.

7. Conclusion

Forming the Boundaries

The recent elections in Azerbaijan have clearly shaped the development of a confrontation line between internal (those in power and the opposition) and external (the West and Russia) political forces. This confrontational nature was present, not only throughout the election process, but also in the assessments of the results and in the responses to the development of post-election trends. The ruling power holds that the elections were conducted in full compliance with international standards, that the requirements of democracy were met, and that the elections were an expression of the will of the Azerbaijani people. The opposition asserts that the elections were totally falsified by the power structures, that the results must be annulled, and that new elections must be held. The course of elections and their results were assessed by international observers in the same contradictory way. In their preliminary assessments, European organisations have stuck to the opinion that the elections did not meet European standards, while the Russian and many CIS observers have talked about the absence of any violations during the election process, and fully approved the position of the Azerbaijani authorities. The impetuous and wavering evolution of the US position is interesting: initially, Washington supported the critical assessments of the OSCE, then recognised the de facto legitimacy of the newly elected parliament and united with the opinion of Moscow and Tehran.

This roughly repeats the familiar situation which took place during the October 2003 presidential elections, with the confrontation between the internal and external positions. But the 2005 situation also has distinctive features, due to the nature of the neo-monarchy and the logical development of the situation. For the first time, the elections were held under the shadow of the 'orange revolution' threat, and were demonstratively falsified for Western eyes, through the use of a counter-revolutionary scenario and with the active participation of Kremlin emissaries. The struggle during the parliamentary elections – concerning the results, and in respect of the political perspectives surrounding Azerbaijan – has been on the highest geopolitical level. Most recently, the tone in this struggle has been set by the Kremlin: this fully suits the neo-Soviet aspirations of the Azerbaijani power, while the West remains in a state of total diplomatic defence.

Relations between Russia and the West

It is notable that the current Russia–West confrontation regarding the nature and results of the election game in Azerbaijan has a background in their competitive joint participation in the formation of the neo-monarchy tradition in 2003. Their increased interest in the recent parliamentary elections can be explained by the fact that both Moscow and Washington were involved in securing the transfer of power from father (Heidar Aliev) to son (Ilham Aliev); naturally, they now feel responsible for the collisions within the neo-monarchy and are competing with each other for the right to control the 'successor'. In the 2003 presidential elections, a radical (neo-monarchic) power transformation took place in the system as such. This pre-determined the development of viewpoints on the political processes in the country, including the correction of its strategic course and the scenario for holding election games. With Ilham Aliev coming to power, the former system, which had a more active pro-Western drift as well as a more consistent imitation of democracy, gave way to 'the model of a competitive geopolitical partnership' between the USA and Russia. This created a pendulum-like motion of Azerbaijan towards the North and towards the West – although, more frequently than not, the country swayed towards the North.

However, the logical development of events, especially the strengthening of the neo-Soviet and pro-Moscow tendencies of the Azerbaijani political course (by the Azerbaijani neo-monarchy) soon forced the White House to take more active and critical measures of influence on official Baku. This can be seen from the fact that, ever since coming into power, Ilham Aliev has yet to be officially invited to Washington. It is likely that the secret US blessing of the 2003 election falsification was made under the condition that Ilham Aliev undertook special obligations, which he then conveniently forgot and started actively working on his friendship with the Kremlin. Increasingly, Washington found such behaviour irritating. On the eve of the 2005 parliamentary elections, the White House began actively using cases of freedom, democracy and even of orange revolution as a means of putting pressure on official Baku, in order to bring the 'lost sheep' of the Azerbaijani neo-monarchy back onto its former pro-Western, pro-US course.

The parliamentary elections revealed the US–Russian disagreement regarding both the nature of the development of geopolitical processes Azerbaijan, and the issue of imposing on the country. The struggle focused on the country's geopolitical future, as well as its political developmental model. The course of the election process and the results of the elections are evidence that, when it comes to the question of the 'pull of the geopolitical rope' between Washington and Moscow, the initiative still belongs to the later.

Sanctions

Immediately after the Azerbaijani Constitutional Court had approved the fraudulent election results, the US Embassy hurriedly gave its agreement with the decision and wished the new parliament success. However, the opinion of the official circles in the Council of Europe remained critical, as before. Within the context of strict declarations made by members of the PACE Monitoring Committee, Leo Platvoet, Andreas Gross and Andres Herkel, complications can be expected in interrelations between official Baku and the Council of Europe, and even the possibility that certain sanctions might be applied towards Azerbaijan. This would indeed seem to be the most serious 'image problem' and the main headache for the Azerbaijani ruling power, who have 'successfully' overcome the other external barriers they faced on the path to legitimisation of the parliament.

The ruling regime of Azerbaijan is scared, not by sanctions, but by the unpredictable influence of the Council of Europe – on the future course of the political processes in the country, and on its development – and also of the possibility of a 'domino effect' that might provoke new punitive measures. Today, the structures of the Council of Europe, and even the powerful USA, do not have at their disposal effective, peaceful sanctions against authoritarian regimes which demonstratively violate democratic demands and have no intention of respecting the recommendations of the West. The political and legal sanctions that are available in their arsenal, used sporadically, contribute to the isolation of such regimes from international community. This in turn only enhances the enforcement of the neo-totalitarian, neo-Soviet, tyrannical tendencies in these countries. In the end, such sanctions can relieve the authoritarian regimes of the burden of the responsibility for fulfilling international norms, thereby making the goal of imitating 'democratic conduct' unnecessary and in reality creating reactionary phenomena. The sanctions predominantly affect not the reactionary regimes themselves, but the people of these countries.

The cases of Belarus and Uzbekistan provide hard confirmation that such sanctions allow authoritarian regimes to extract maximum positive dividends for themselves. We may assume that new leadership of Azerbaijan will view the possible sanctions of the West not as real and dangerous threats, but as a discomforting and yet useful good that in effect furthers the goals of neo-Soviet power. The present leadership of Azerbaijan, in its own pro-Russian drift and neo-Soviet goals, has travelled too far for Western sanctions to scare it much or provide a corrective influence on its political course. However, in the end, this may prove to be the biggest and most dangerous blunder of all.

USA and Europe: Polarised Perspectives

Whether or not this is the case, the potential collisions in the political situation in Azerbaijan will depend not only on the developmental process inside the country, but on the reaction of the West to the clearly undemocratic Azerbaijani power – prior to and during the parliamentary elections. At present, the co-ordinated or un-co-ordinated polarisation of opinion between the USA and Europe is being felt. The position of the former was expressed in its embassy press release: 'The USA intends to co-operate closely with the newly elected Parliament of Azerbaijan.' Many voices can be heard in this statement: the independents, the opposition, and the ruling party. The European position was once again expressed by the members of the PACE Monitoring Committee: 'We believe that such a parliament cannot be considered to be an authentic representative body. What is a parliament without an opposition? The political situation in Azerbaijan raises deep concern. If this condition remains, then the population will lose all trust in democratic institutes.' Furthermore, European parliamentarians expressed surprise over the position of Washington: 'The current position of the United States means Bush's refusal to stand by his own statements made during his inauguration. He once declared that democracy and human rights were to be his priorities, but he applies two-faced standards to their meaning. We hope that Europe will stand by these principles.'

In reality, democratic society in Azerbaijan can rely only on the fact that Europe will be more principled in this regard, and will not let geopolitical, oil, and other pragmatic interests triumph over the interests of freedom, democracy, and human rights. If, once again, the response to the Aliev regime's imitation of democracy is yet another imitation of democratic support (by the official West), this may have highly negative consequences for the development of democratic processes in Azerbaijan. On the one hand, this may free the hands of the corrupted neo-Soviet power regime, providing it with an impulse to continue on the harsh authoritarian course aimed at crushing freedom and democracy even more. On the other hand, this may mean the end of the democratic and pro-Western expectations of society, impelling many citizens to reconcile before reaction – or, alternatively, impelling them to seek support in other directions or in other forms of struggle. Such perspectives are not in the interest of Azerbaijani democratic society, nor are they likely to correspond with the interests of the international democratic society.

IV   THE 2005 PARLIAMENTARY ELECTIONS: A MIRROR OF POLITICS AND SOCIETY IN AZERBAIJAN

Zardusht Alizade

1. Introduction: Election Process in Azerbaijan

On 6 November 2005 events took place in Azerbaijan that the government called the 'elections' to the parliament (the National Assembly). The opposition, seeing these elections as a farce and an act of violence against the will of the electorate, sought to express its protest through the courts and through mass rallies. The courts dismissed all these civil suits, and the police used violence to break up the rallies. All attempts to question the results of the elections (in the streets and squares, as had taken place in Georgia, Ukraine and Kyrgyzstan) were nipped in the bud by the regime. The Aliev clan and the ruling political class retained control over the powerless parliament.

Both the ruling party and the opposition were preparing for a political battle: not just for the parliament, but just as much for overall power. No one concealed the fact that what was at stake was *all* power in the country – including presidential power. In the print media and in speeches by opposition leaders, parallels were drawn with the situation in Georgia, where elections had resulted in the removal of President Edward Shevardnadze.

The ruling party had begun to mobilise all its administrative resource for the parliamentary elections long before 2005, in order to prepare for the elections (or, as the opposition press called it, the 'special police operation').

The Controlled Election Process

Central Election Commission (CEC)
In Azerbaijan, the ruling party has full control over the country's election system. The CEC consisted of 15 members: five elected by the party with the parliamentary majority, *Jeny Azerbaijan* (the pocket party of the Aliev family); five elected as a result of the voting by the so-called independent deputies of the National Assembly (who were, in reality, part of the ruling power); and five elected by the parties of the parliamentary opposition. Of the latter five, (members considered to be the defenders of interests of opposition), three were representatives of the parties of the National Independence, the People's Front. The Democratic Party had signed the final minutes of the totally fraudulent presidential elections in 2003; it is for this reason that they were considered, within the opposition environment, to be 'people bribed by power'. Only two members of the CEC – the representatives of Musavat and Civil Solidarity – tried to call on the CEC, as the highest election body, to observe the law during the organisation of the elections, but this had no effect.

Territorial Election Commissions and Voter Statistics
The territorial election commissions were formed on the basis of the same principles as the polling station commissions. Each of the 5,127 polling station commissions established during parliamentary elections of 2005 consisted of six members: a total of 30,762 people. The country was divided into 125 constituencies with an average population of approximately 40,000 voters.

CEC Activity
During the first years of independence, the CEC decided to organise elections in the 122nd Stepankertski constituency of Nagorny Karabah. This territory has a majority Armenian population and is in fact under the control of the army of the Republic of Armenia and of the armed forces of the unrecognised Republic of Nagorny Karabah. The democratic republic of Azerbaijan welcomed this CEC step as a sign of its preparedness to take part in reconciliation and dialogue. However, the awkward way in which this decision was announced reduced its positive potential to near zero. During the elections in

this constituency, only 9,000 Azerbaijani citizens participated; they had suffered during the ethnic cleansing that took place Stepanokert in September 1988. The Armenian population did not express any view on the decision of the Azerbaijani CEC. Furthermore, the separatist regime of the Nagorny Karabah publicly rejected the possibility of any participation by the Armenian population in the elections, which concerned a deputy to the parliament of Azerbaijan.

Election Commissions: A Compromised Position
Altogether, 31,912 Azerbaijani citizens were members of the commissions at various levels. They were, for the most part, employees from the budgetary sphere, teachers, doctors, and clerical and ordinary workers. These members were materially dependant (because they receive public sector salaries) on the authorities and did not have the slightest protection from the arbitrary rule of the executive power, whether in the courts, or in the corrupt 'yellow' trade unions. Naturally, this army of over 30,000 people was operated by the heads of the various district executive powers, and through the enforcement structures (the Ministry of Interior Affairs and National Security), whose employees were always involved in the elections – which, in turn, had the aim of protecting the Aliev family.

Although the Election Code prohibits executive level and enforcement structure staff from taking part in the activities of Election Commissions, this legal prohibition has always been violated in practice. All complaints made by the opposition (and independent) candidates of legal violations are ignored by the ruling power.

Additional Pressure from the President
The late President, Heidar Aliev, encouraged the violation of election laws by commission members, and ensured their impunity. After each election (accompanied by mass legal violations), he would issue a decree on amnesty; this would neatly include the articles of the laws that stipulated the administrative and criminal violations of the election laws. In this way, Heidar Aliev would ensure that the members of the election commissions and the staff of the executive power bodies clearly understood that nothing could threaten them for violating the laws, as long as they remained faithful to him. His son,

Ilham Aliev, went even farther: after the 2005 parliamentary elections, those heads of the Territorial Election Commissions who had not been able to falsify the elections, and who produced the final minutes to the opposition candidates effectively affirming their victory, were made 'criminally responsible'.

The Opposition: Growing Support

Following the Ukrainian Example
The opposition thoroughly studied the experience of the 'orange' revolutions in Georgia and Ukraine. Additionally, it established co-operation with youth organisations in those countries, as these had played an important role in the victory of the opposition. The US-based National Democracy Institute (NDI) (which works closely together with the national-democratic wing of the opposition) financed a tour for a large group of Azerbaijani democratic movement activists to attend the Ukrainian elections in 2004. Courses were organised for them there, during which they studied the election laws of Ukraine, as well as other specifics of the Ukrainian election process. This team (which observed the elections in Eastern Ukraine, and which later submitted valuable reports regarding violations of laws during voting), gained considerable practical experience of election monitoring, which they then shared with activists from the 'Azadlyg' ('Freedom') bloc.

Other Helping Hands
Apart from this, the NGO Centre for the Monitoring of Elections (supported by the NDI) was preparing to monitor the elections. The authorities of Azerbaijan would not allow the NDI itself to monitor the elections during the Presidential Elections of 2003, nor in the 2005 Parliamentary Elections.

The Soros Foundation also announced a tender for NGOs, aimed at educating the electorate as to their rights and responsibilities. Such Western-source funds for voter education and the provision of civil society control over the elections were generally scarce. They were met with hostility from authorities in Azerbaijan; the government mass media began spreading a thesis, in the spirit of the Soviet 'agitprop' (agitation and propaganda), on the 'intrigues of the West against the independence of Azerbaijan'.

The State against Society
In other recent elections in Azerbaijan, the political opposition parties and NGOs undertook active measures only in the last stages of the election process – and ended up with timing problems. This time, civil society, including parties and NGOs, started preparations for the elections somewhat earlier. Nevertheless, many analysts predicted that the Georgian and the Ukrainian election scenarios would not be repeated in Azerbaijan. They believe that the situation in Azerbaijan was radically different from that in Georgia and Ukraine. There was in fact a central difference between Azerbaijani domestic policy and the policies of the 'coloured revolutions' countries: in those countries, the split had occurred *within* the ruling political class (i.e. confrontation between various groups in the parliament and in the government), whereas in Azerbaijan, the battle was between 'shacks and palaces', between the streets and the offices of power. In Azerbaijan, the ruling political class met Election Day as a united team, having already rid themselves of those who were ready to desert to the camp of the opposition. For this reason, the struggle on Election Day was based on the traditional scheme of 'the government against the people' and 'the government against society'. The result was equally traditional: the government won, society lost.

2. Election Process in Azerbaijan

CIS Countries and Democracy: General Attitudes

In all Commonwealth of Independent States (CIS) countries, the ruling elites, to a greater or lesser degree, have a hostile attitude towards democracy and its institutes – and towards free, transparent and fair elections in particular. Of all former Soviet republics, only the elections in Estonia, Lithuania and Latvia correspond to European standards

'Guided Democracy'
In the CIS countries, the powerful elite can be replaced only through revolutionary violence, and this can occur only when an adequate force is positioned against the political structure. This means the force of the crowds in the streets. The presidents in these countries dominate all branches of power. To prevent loss of power during elections, they mobilise all the state's resources against the people, whilst systematically weakening the opposition in the inter-election period by cutting it off from financial, administrative and information resources. The state is waging a war against civil society, hypocritically disguising its actions under the vague term of 'guided democracy'.

Taking the Lion's Share
The main reason for such hostility and irreconcilability between the government and the people lies in the nature of the attitude of officialdom towards property. The ruling Azerbaijan bourgeoisie is not a trade and manufacturing bourgeoisie, but an officialdom bourgeoisie, a class of governmental bureaucrats. Their source and means of income rest in their position in the governmental apparatus. The pyramidal governmental machine of independent Azerbaijan is ideally structured to allow the appropriation of the lion's share of budget and oil revenues by a small elite group – primarily the family of President Aliev, his relatives, friends, fellows, ministers, deputies and top official in the regions.

Protecting Personal Economic Interests: Mechanisms of State Control
A system of 'collective cover-ups' connects all members of the ruling elite: they use all the means of the repressive governmental machine to protection their own economic interests, and this in a very cohesive manner. Any attempt by the people to apply to the courts, prosecutors' offices, or other governmental entities are met by the mocking words of officials: 'Go, complain to anyone you want!' In fact there is no independent and fair court in Azerbaijan. Despite all the efforts of the OSCE and the CoE, the authorities have 'reformed' the country's judiciary system so that all judges have become directly and heavily dependent on the executive power, and must work under its dictates.

Even though there are formally 'private and independent' TV channels, television is fully under control of the relevant unit of the Office of the President. Most of the press has been bribed. Opposition newspapers have a measly circulation and eke out a miserable existence because the authorities have prohibited businesses from placing advertisements in these newspapers. Any businessman who is close to the opposition is put under pressure from the government's controlling bodies. For this reason, opposition parties and candidates are able to mobilise only meagre funds for elections, unlike the funding available to the government parties. The ruling powers are waging all-out warfare against civil society. They discredit and bribe NGOs through the use of skilful pressure – blackmailing them and threatening to prohibit their activities (similar to what has happened in Russia, Belarus and Uzbekistan), and getting international funds to reduce their financial support to rebellious NGOs.

All information about the real owners of private companies (incomes, profits, financial flows, contracts and credits) is held as the strictest of state secrets. The State Statistical Committee publishes distorted, manipulated information. Over half of the country's economy is kept in the shadow. Budget funds, credits, and grants are siphoned off by top officials. Any attempts by civil society at achieving greater transparency are firmly quelled.

Protection of Personal Economic Interests and the Elections
The nature of the public relations described above, whereby power is used as a means of privatising the lion's share of public revenues, is the reason why

the ruling class cannot allow fair and equitable elections to be carried out in compliance with the Copenhagen principles. Democratic elections would inevitably bring the opposition to power, as shown every time there has been an expert assessment of the elections. But expert assessments are not official juridical documents, with the validity for confirming the results of the voting. Such documents are routinely falsified by the ruling power, in its own favour.

Temperament of the Ruling Class

From the moment Heidar Aliev came to power in Azerbaijan in 1969, the process for selecting the ruling elite started to be based on negative characteristics. The main asset of those striving for prosperity in the state became their ability to adapt to the whims of the heads, rather than their devotion to laws and morals. Giving priority to local interests, nepotism, corruption, and collective cover-ups became the law of the life of the elite.

Criminal Tendencies

After the return of Heidar Aliev to power in 1993, the 'criminalisation of those in power' (including murders on orders from higher up) and strict property stratification were added to this list. In 1994, Afiyaddin Jalilov, deputy-Speaker of the parliament, and Shamsi Ragimov, head of the special department on security issues under the President, were killed, as were M.P. Ali Antsuhskiy in 1996, and Ziya Buniatov, Vice-President on ruling parties, M.P., hero of the Soviet Union and academician) in 1997. Responsibility for these murders was cast on the Prime Minister (then out of favour), the foreign intelligence services and the Islamists. However, opinion within society holds that the hidden interests of inter-power groups lie behind these murders and coup d'etat performances. The rapid enrichment of members of the ruling family and the equally swift impoverishment of much of the population became so obvious that it was noted by Rasim Gasanov, Director of the Centre of Economic Reforms under the Ministry of Economic Development, in his fundamental research. Gasanov points out: 'In 1990, 5% of the population with the highest incomes were receiving 6.2% of the total revenue. In 1993, this figure increased to 22.8%, and in 1997 to 61.5%.'[1] Those disloyal to the President were forced out of the ruling elite. All the Special Services focused on undertaking subversive activities, directed against the opposition and civil society. Disloyalty to the suzerain, rather than the embezzlement of public funds, became a crime. The President started to encourage corruption and simultaneously began to compile compromising material on officials. Soon there were no untainted and independent members left in the elite. The nature of power became criminal, and to join the circles of power began to mean to become a criminal, or at least become reconciled to crime.

Heidar Aliev
Heidar Aliev, KGB General, member of Politburo of the CPSU CC, and a politician, had been brought up within the totalitarian school of the CPSU and KGB. He was one of the later leaders of the Soviet regime, for whom the highest award was recognition as a team-mate 'politician of Lenin's type'. He accurately reconstructed the Soviet system of power in independent Azerbaijan. Under the guise of being the President of Azerbaijan, he became the uncontrolled 'General Secretary of the CPSU CC'. He entrusted the Office of the President with the functions of CPSU CC, curtailing the authority of the Cabinet of Ministers even more than had been with case the Council of Ministers of the USSR. He also accorded only nominal rights to the Supreme Council of the 'National Assembly'.

Power and the People
Such power, naturally, must structure its relations with the people. This was done in the same manner as the relationship of a rapist with his victim. The foundation of the power became corruption for the elite, violence and deceit for the people, and demagogy for the international community.

---

1   Gasanoc, R.T. Conceptual frameworks of market model of socio-economic development of the Azerbaijan Republic (in the Azerbaijan language) Baku. Elm. 1998.

3. The Nature of the Opposition

History

The Popular Front of Azerbaijan
The main leaders and activists of the opposition parties in Azerbaijan are, by origin, from the Popular Front of Azerbaijan, a party coloured by its composition as a people's movement. During the decline of the Communist Party of the Soviet Union, all communists were called 'democrats'; fascist-minded nationalists and the mob, craving for power, with only the slightest notion of democracy, were also considered anti-communists and democrats. The Popular Front, which took power in May 1992 and ruled for one year only, represented a classic example of ochlocracy, without the slightest democratic governance skills. This became the main reason for their power loss. Twelve years of being in the opposition resulted in the movement splitting into several mutually hostile parties.

The Opposition and the Ruling Power
Relations between the national-democratic opposition and those in power were (and still are) of a clandestine nature, with the tribal Nahichevan-Armenistan wing of the ruling political class and the ostentatious, irreconcilable front designed for the naive masses. During the 2005 parliamentary elections, this became apparent in a peculiar way. The tribal union had already come into power in 1993, practically monopolising control over the country's financial, economic, administrative and information resources. Thereupon the national democrats allied with those in the clan who craved a power take-over from the ruling Aliev family. This is the reason behind the union of the two national-democratic parties (the Popular Front and the Musavat with the Democratic Party). The leader of this union, Rasul Guliev, had been the main financier of the Heidar Aliev campaign for power, as well as Speaker of the parliament under Aliev between 1993 and 1996.

Internal Rivalry

The spirit of rivalry prevailed against the spirit of co-operation, within the Azadlyg bloc and between the two opposition blocs (Azadlyg and the 'YES'- 'New Policy' union). When, on the eve of elections, the YES bloc proposed to the Azadlyg bloc that they might sub-divide constituencies in order to avoid rivalry between their candidates, the national-democrats responded that they could let them have only two constituencies. YES could not accept such a proposal, so nothing came of the agreement. The candidates of two opposi- tional blocs had to compete against each other in many constituencies.

'YES' is the bloc in which many former leaders of the country united, includ- ing:

- Ayaz Mutalibov, President of Azerbaijan 1990–1992;
- Yagub Mamedov, former chairperson of the parliament and acting President of the Republic in 1992;
- Rahim Huseynov, Prime Minister 1992–1993;
- Ali Masimov, acting Prime Minister in 1993;
- Vahid Ahmedov, former Vice Prime Minister;
- Etibar Mamedov, former presidential candidate in 1998;
- Eldar Namazov, former assistant to the President.

Issues Impeding the Establishment of a Democratic Coalition

Dominant Points of View

Discussion of the co-ordination efforts by various opposition parties on estab- lishing a broad democratic coalition during elections has generally been lim- ited by the framework created by two points of view widespread in the public conscience of Azerbaijan.

The one is based on a romantic, community perception that sees the peo- ple as a whole, and proposes uniting all opposition forces for the sake of 'the sacred all-national objectives' (fair elections, liberation of occupied lands, overthrow of the traitorous power, etc). This point of view fails to grasp the real difference of interests between the various groups in population, and the impossibility of organising these political forces, with their varying levels of strength and influence, in the absence of efficient democratic mechanisms and skills.

The second point of view highlights the availability of structurally and functionally capable parties with ambitious leaders. It holds that society should unite around these parties and, if a situation occurs whereby a significant part of the anti-government population does not accept or even rejects them, this should be ignored. Proponents of this view point out that, prior to every election, there are heated debates around the ideas, forms, and goals of such a coalition, yet this never ends in the establishment of a truly wide bloc. Moreover, the leaders of the 'democratic' camp are authoritarian to the same degree: they are closed to society and avoid transparency in the same manner as the officials do. Any negotiations between the leaders of the parties begin with the signing of a 'gentleman's agreement' on the non-disclosure of the details of the negotiations. However, because journalists have long since lost their piety to leaders of the opposition, all these negotiations are commented on. In the mass media, the commentary is done in an ironic manner and always includes some comical details, as well as providing evidence of the lack of foresight and greediness of these leaders. Mehriban Vezir (journalist, member of the Administration of the Party of the Popular Front (the classics) and MP candidate), who won a convincing election victory but who was not allowed into the parliament due to falsification of the voting results by the Territorial Election Commission, wrote about general atmosphere in the opposition and the reasons why attempts to unite its various detachments had failed.[2]

Other Careless Practices

The carelessness of the leaders of the 'Azadlyg' bloc meant that several well-known opposition activists were not entered on the single list of candidates co-ordinated by three parties. They were nominated as independent deputies and had to compete for the vote of the protesting electorate with less-known candidates of the bloc. As a result, the opposition lost in these constituencies.

---

2   Vezir, M. 'Dangerous, unhappy, sad Azerbaijan' (in Azeri language), from the newspaper *Baku Xeber,* 30 December 2005.

For example, in the centre of Baku (where most voters were non-manual workers, teachers and doctors), instead of supporting Rasim Musabekov (a well-known political scientist and member of the Musavat administration), the Azadlyg bloc supported a little-known provincial, Zamina Dunyamaliyeva, from the Democratic Party. Rashid Gadzhly, a famous lawyer and candidate of the 'YES' bloc, was also running in that constituency. As a result, having divided the votes of the protesting electorate, they took third, fourth and fifth place.

The Opposition: a General Note

On the whole, the history of the national-democratic opposition, as well as its character and the conduct of its leaders, has not led towards co-operation and reconciliation. The benchmarks of the political struggle of the national democrats include highlighting banned methods, bloody collisions, riots, and overthrowing those political leaders who actually rejected the repression and started working together with them. This is one reason why power always applies illegal methods in order to suppress this.

4. The People

Not only in Azerbaijan, but also in Russia, Kazakhstan, Armenia and other CIS countries, a core part of the population is indifferent to politics and prefers the sidelines. It becomes possible to radicalise population only when there is a split within the ruling political class. Additionally, in order for this radicalisation to occur, one must significantly target (and thus support) the financial, administrative and information resources of the opposition. In the 2003 Azerbaijan presidential elections this did not happen, and the population quietly accepted the fact that the election had been so roughly falsified. They did not support the acts of protest by national-democrats.

The poorest section of the population is scattered in the villages of the provinces and is not capable of self-organisation. In towns, the few operating enterprises (with their large worker collectives) pay their employees comparatively high salaries, which generates political indifference amongst the workers. Small retailers and day labourers are tied to their work places because of the necessity of earning a daily living, and cannot participate in protest actions. With rare exceptions, meetings of opposition have been attended by members of the parties, the unemployed, and clerks, who suffer most of all from the injustice of the State.

5. The Election Process in Action

Long before the parliamentary elections, people had realised that these elections would be held in compliance with the regulations of the Election Code. It was also known that the Aliev family party, Jeni Azerbaijan, would secure the majority of places in all levels of the election commissions.

The Opposition and Election Code Amendments: Failed Attempt

At the beginning of 2005, the opposition started campaigning for the introduction of Election Code amendments that would secure it equal standing within the election commissions. The campaign was held in both the press and amongst the population, as well as within the leading Western international organisations in Baku. The OSCE and EC supported the requirements of the opposition. Negotiations were also held between the representatives of these organisations and the ruling party. However, President Ilham Aliev put an end to these attempts to achieve equality in the election commissions, reminding people that the opposition had used parity in 2000 in order to sabotage the work of the CEC (he neglected to mention that the reason for this 'sabotage' was that the ruling party had intended to ignore the opinion of the opposition so as to retain control over the CEC). Thereafter, the opposition presented this equality requirement as one of its main demands. Despite this, the absence of a threat of election boycott (from the opposition) gave the ruling party full confidence that its unwillingness to seek a compromise would, in the end, be accepted both domestically and abroad. The section of the Election Code covering the composition of commissions was not amended. Some amendments were introduced into other articles, but these were insignificant for the elections.

The Opposition: Preventing Falsification

On the whole, the opposition was getting prepared not so much for the elections, but for preventing any falsification of the results. At the 2003 presidential elections, the CEC had removed 30% of the votes from the main opposition candidate and endorsed them to Ilham Aliev.[3] Actions protesting were brutally suppressed. An unofficial moratorium on meetings was introduced for a period of almost a year and a half. For these reasons, the opposition and civil society were getting prepared to rebuff and struggle. They conducted enhanced training of observers and members of the opposition in the commissions, teaching them to draw up acts, and providing studies of the experience of previous elections in Azerbaijan and in Ukraine in 2004.

Reports of the Co-ordinating Advisory Council (CAC)

In the 2003 presidential and 2004 municipal elections, civil society was united within the framework of the Co-ordinating Advisory Council (CAC), which included over 40 NGOs. Based on the results of the elections, uniform co-ordinated reports were prepared. International organisations referred to these during their assessment of the elections in Azerbaijan.

The Reports
The CAC reports clearly showed that the election victory was with the opposition. They also noted how the ruling party had used all means to obstruct the process of obtaining reliable data, with extensive use of violence, intimidation and unfair shuffling. Due to the absence of reliable data, supported by unshuffled documents, the CAC alleged that the elections data which had been received did not confirm the victory of the ruling power candidates. However, for the same reason, the data were also insufficient for confirming the victory of the opposition.

Subsequent Reactions
This objective position caused discontent among both the ruling powers and the opposition. The former were angry that their illegal activities were being recorded at many polling stations and constituencies, and were brought to the attention of public opinion within the country and abroad, while the opposition was receiving unconditional loyalty from the NGOs, seeing itself as a symbol of democracy. For this reason, perhaps, some ten NGOs who were close to

---

3   From the newspaper *Azadlyg*, 10 and 11 November 2005.

the national democrats had withdrawn from CAC on the eve of the election process, and announced the establishment of a new coalition –'Golden Autumn'. This coalition soon splintered, but its campaign on the defamation of civil society, within the pages of governmental press and television, was actively carried out.

The opposition tried to introduce democratic rules for the selection of candidates in the single list, although this did not take place everywhere. However, as the results demonstrated, the opposition did not succeed in learning democratic norms. Furthermore, with regard to bright names, the rosters of the opposition were generally poor. Likewise for the rosters of the ruling power, which contained the administration of the party 'Jeni Azerbaijan' (which had received their mandates as a result of the scandalous falsification of the parliamentary elections in 1995 and 2000), and along with this were several new faces, whose names had been mentioned by the press in connection with misappropriation of loans and monopolisation of various spheres of the economy. There were perhaps ten educated and intelligent people who could be considered to be the exceptions; they had been included in the list in the hope that they might become representatives in European structures.

Party Roster and Other Tactics

Self-nomination
It was known in advance that a certain part of this roster would be sacrificed, by the ruling power itself, in order to create a semblance of democracy. Aside from those included on the party roster, hundreds of members of the ruling party were self-nominated: this was presented as a victory for democracy. However, an analysis of the situation in the constituencies, along with the cancellation of the requirement of a quorum, showed that, by doing this, the party Jeni Azerbaijan tried to apply some new techniques. Knowing that the forces of the ruling power and of the opposition were approximately equal, the party did not oppose the self-nomination by hundreds of its members, counting on the fact that they would not be able to attract undecided voters. The average Azerbaijani voter has a strongly developed sense of priority to local interests, as well as nepotism and a client-focused attitude. In order to prevent an opposition candidate from winning over undecided voters, the ruling

party decided to disintegrate and group around its own numerous candidates, each of whom could gain up to 100 votes from relatives, neighbours and friends.

Annulled Registrations

This expectation, however, proved wrong. Confidential elections polling showed that, in a sizeable number of constituencies, candidates for the ruling power were losing badly to the opposition and needed the maximum mobilisation of all their resources. Those in power then started to twist the arms of their own allies so as to have only one ruling power representative left on the list. Seeking to clear the election field for their own candidates, the ruling power also dared to annul the registration of several opposition and independent candidates. On the eve of the elections, the total number of registrations annulled by the CEC and in the courts was a full 351. The greatly praised figure of 2,062 candidates, which was held to demonstrate the 'blossoming of democracy' in the country, fell to 1,711. Some candidates (members of the ruling party lodged within the number of 'unofficial' and independent ones) lost around 1 million dollars each at the initial stage of the election campaign, before they were forced to retract their candidatures due to threats.

General Statistics

A record number of candidates to a single seat became a distinctive feature of the parliamentary elections of 2005. The lowest number of candidates was registered in Saatly constituency, where the 80-year-old brother of the late President Heidar Aliev was running (the scientist Jalal Aliev). Annangi Gadjibeli, a member of the People's Front Party and a lawyer, had the courage to challenge the uncle of the current President for the third time. Naturally, the president's uncle won. A large number of candidates (36 in fact) were registered in Binagady constituency of Baku city, where Sardar Jalaloglu, general secretary of the Democratic Party, was running. By Election Day, only 21 candidates were left, over whom Jalaloglu won: however the CEC refused to approve his victory and annulled the election results in this constituency.

6. Candidate Registration

Traditional Impediments

The initial period from 5 July to final registration was characterised by various impediments created by those in power to obstruct independent and opposi- tional candidates.

Targeting the Islamic Parties
They were particularly zealous in respect of the Muslims and the Democratic Party. Although they did not have the official status of mullah, several promi- nent Muslim scholars were not allowed to register, with reference to the rule that a servant of a religious cult cannot be engaged in politics.

Initially, the leader of the Islamic Party of Azerbaijan, Hajiaga Nuriev, was registered. Then, having learned of the wide support that Nuriev enjoyed in his constituency, the CEC allowed a petition on the annulment of his registra- tion, submitted by a CEC member from the Musavat Party. In this way, the member was trying to pave the way for the editor-in-chief of the newspaper *Jeni Musavat*, Rauf Arifoglu. Despite numerous appeals by the Muslim leader and by courts of various instances, the decision to annul his registration re- mained left in force. After the elections, Nuriev filed a court case against the CEC member in question for damaging his reputation, but no court decision would be able to make an impact on the approved results of the elections.

Rasul Guliev
A somewhat strange registration came from the out-of-favour ex-Speaker Ra- sul Guliev, who had immigrated to the USA. The Territorial Election Commis- sion refused to issue lists for the collection of signatures by persons empow- ered to act for him, on the grounds that he did not have an ID as a citizen of Azerbaijan, and also because he bore responsibility to a foreign government, as a taxpayer to the US budget. Activists of Azerbaijan's Democratic Party began to panic, having telephoned their leader in the USA to inform him of the failure. Rasul Guliev calmed them down and promised that he would push certain levers, and that it would work; just a day later, a phone call was made

from the Territorial Election Commission to the Democratic Party, asking them to come and pick lists for the collection of the signatures. In only two days the necessary number of signatures had been collected and submitted to the Territorial Election Commission. All the same, the registration experienced new delays. When all the terms as defined by legislation had expired, members of the Democratic Party once again called made a call to the USA and informed Rasul Guliev about the new impediment. The leader of Democrats pressed the necessary buttons: one day later, the activists of the Democratic Party were invited to the Territorial Election Commission, where they delivered a document certifying that Rasul Guliev was registered as a candidate in the forthcoming elections.

Removing the Impediments

After some time, an order was issued by the CEC, and all the impediments placed in the way of the candidates' registration were removed. As a result, during the second stage of the pre-election campaign, 2,062 candidates joined in the competition for 125 mandates. Later, however, 351 of these withdrew, either voluntarily or by force, leaving only 1,711 candidates in the end.

7. The Pre-Election Campaign Stage

Election Campaign Tactics

'Charitable Activity'

By law, the formal election campaign is to start 60 days prior to the elections – in this case, 7 September. However, both the ruling power and the opposition began campaigning long before this date. Rich candidates started broad charitable activity, as well as construction and improvement work. Naturally, nobody called these activities 'the election campaign'. Money was distributed to poor families, refugees, pensioners, orphans and orphanages. Schools were rehabilitated, roads and yards asphalted, transformers installed, cables and pipes laid. Magnificent weddings and free meals were organised. Religious holidays were celebrated. In honour of the Commemoration Day of the Shiite Martyr, ruling-power candidates as well as atheists and embezzlers of public funds were found organising sumptuous free meals, to which hundreds of voters came.

Protest Meetings

The opposition could not afford to be so lavish, and focused instead on protest meetings. The main demand at meetings during the spring/summer of 2005 was assuring parity in the election commissions. However, both the opposition and the representatives of international organisations came to realise that those in power would not agree to amend the Election Code to guarantee parity in the formation of commissions. Meetings became increasingly radicalised, with impassioned speeches on the necessity of dismissing 'the corrupt, thieves, law violators, and betrayers of the people's interests'. It was clear that the speakers were referring to all the elite in power, but most of all to the executive power.

The Return of the President

In late August, having registered as candidates, ex-President Ayaz Mutallibov, and ex-Speaker Rasul Guliev announced that they were preparing to return to Azerbaijan to take part in the direct conduct of their election campaigns.

The response of the authorities came with lightning speed; upon the presentation of the general prosecutor's office, the courts of Azerbaijan annulled the status of immunity to which all election candidates were entitled by law. Both the Minister of Internal Affairs, Ramil Usubov, and the General Prosecutor, Zakir Garalov, vowed to arrest Ayaz Mulallibov and Rasul Guliev as soon as they set foot on Azerbajani soil. In response, the national-democratic opposition relocated its meetings to the central squares of the capital.

The National Democratic Meeting Movement

Short-Lived Meetings in Azadlyg Square
The National Democrat Meeting Movement, begun during the 1988–1991 period of USSR disintegration, having started in the central Azadlyg ('Freedom') Square in Baku) was growing like an avalanche and absorbing all the protesting population. Earlier, it had been responsible for overthrowing the leaders of the country – Abdul-Rakman Vezirov in 1990 and Ayaz Mutallibov in 1992. Heidar Aliev, who had actively assisted members of 'The Front', took into account the danger of the meetings in Azadlyg Square. By assigning to the main square the legal status of a place reserved for official governmental events, he provided formal grounds for the head of the executive power of Baku to refuse to requests from the opposition to hold meetings there. Other central squares of Baku were also closed, under the pretext of 'intensive traffic flows' and 'possible disturbance for those living in the neighbouring houses'.

Finding an Alternative Venue
For meetings, the opposition power allocated a small square in front of the former movie theatre 'Gelebe', or 'Victory' (where the State Movie Fund is currently located), on a permanent basis. This square can accommodate no more than five thousand people. When the crowd fills in the neighbouring streets, the number of people can increase by four times this number. In this square, the opposition held several meetings, with the number of participants continuously growing. The leaders announced that the meeting of 9 October

would take place in the centre of the city, in the square near the railway station. The authorities took this decision as signalling the start of an 'orange revolution'. Permission for holding a meeting in the centre of the city on 9 October was not issued, under a skimpy pretext. The Azadlyg bloc then decided to hold the meeting anyway, and called on its allies for support.

Violent Repression

Several thousand people dared to attend that forbidden meeting. Besides the police forces, the ruling power brought in fighters from private armies, bodyguards, and the security forces of private companies. On 9 October these forces not only tried to break up the meeting, but did their best to brutally beat the demonstrators. They beat them with rubber batons, wooden sticks and even brass knuckles.[4] The meeting was dispersed and the people were beaten, maimed and frightened.

The broken rally on 9 October and the terror and violence shown by the ruling power against the demonstrators became a turning point in the 2005 election campaign. It showed there would be no opportunity for the opposition to prevent the authorities from carrying out the elections based on their scenario. From Rasul Guliev came an announcement of his return to Baku on 17 October. On 17 October those in power unexpectedly blocked two roads leading to the airport and preventively arrested several hundred activists of the Democratic Party. Leaders of the Azadlyg bloc did not even try to break through, to get to the airport in order to meet their ally.

The Detention of Rasul Guliev

The private plane on which Rasul Guliev flew from London to Baku was not allowed to land, and Guliev was forced to turn back. He then boarded a plane at the airport of Simferopol in Ukraine, but was detained at the request of Azerbaijan, and handed over to Interpol. However, several days later he was released because Azerbaijan did not present the court with the evidence and documents of his crime necessary for his extradition. Released from deten-

---

4   *Azadlyg*, 10 and 11 November 2005.

tion, Guliev then flew to Kiev, from Kiev to London, and then to the USA. Though he promised to return, nobody took this seriously.

Being arrested is not advantageous for anybody, nor is having the court against you. Naturally, as a former companion-in-arms of Heidar Aliev, Rasul Guliev knew best of all the true value of the Azerbaijani court. This is why he had every reason to assume that having the court against him would be a mere show of reprisals of the Aliev family against a competitor claiming oil profits. On the other hand, an arrest would not have been in the interest of the Aliev family, nor would it be in their interest to turn the court against him – because, as a well-informed person, Guliev could disclose many incriminating secrets of the political and financial affairs of the ruling family during the court hearing.

Other Notable Arrests
After the incident involving Rasul Guliev, the ruling power carried out arrests among his brothers-in-arms (both supposed and real ones), including:

- Ministers of Health and Economic Development, Ali Insanov and Farhad Aliev;
- Chairperson of the state company 'Azrchemia', Fikret Sadyhov;
- Managing head of the presidential administration, Akif Muradverdiev;
- Ex-President of the Academy of Sciences, Eldar Salayev;
- and several other top-level officials.

TV broadcasts were made showing the glamorous palaces of the ministers, of the tens of kilogrammes of gold and precious stones, as well as the millions of dollars and euros. A campaign began against a group of 'rebels who were preparing a coup d'etat', backed by the threat of future arrests and presented as a pledge from those in power, to carry out wide-scale arrests among the leaders of the opposition. As a result, the leaders toned down their radicalism.

Re-Establishing the Opposition

After the events leading to the failure of the Azadlyg bloc, the leaders of the bloc announced on 17 October that they had relocated the centre of the political struggle into the territories. By that time, the correlation of forces was already known, and the ruling power began urgently annulling the registration of opposition activists within the second tier, as these could win over candidates from the ruling power. The Balaken independent candidate, Khalilov Khalid, was forced to withdraw his own candidature, and an opposition member, Gunduzov Osman, withdrew his own candidature for CEC elections, without providing any reason. The election field was prepared for the 'convincing' victory of the candidate of the ruling power, Rabiyat Aslanova.

The leader of the Azadlyg bloc began travelling throughout the country, organising meetings. In many places the ruling power created illegitimate impediments and, in those places where meetings were permitted, they were not able to make a significant impact on the course of events.

TV Campaigns

A more effective method was TV campaigning. Candidates from the registered political parties and blocs, who nominated candidates in over half of the constituencies, were provided with free time on the air, whereas independent candidates had to pay for broadcasting time themselves. Representatives of the Azadlyg bloc sharply and violently criticised this policy. In their address to the ruling power in general, and to its selected candidates, the tirades noticeably activated the protesting electorate, which was one reason why the electorate consolidated around the 'orange' candidates.

Expenditure

During the 2005 elections, civil society was not able to fulfil the legal requirements on transparency of its expenditures during the election campaign. The state allocated approximately USD 220 to each candidate. By law, the upper ceiling for election campaign expenditures was set to USD 86,000. Some opposition and independent candidates spent far more than the amount allocated by the state. However, most candidates from the ruling power spent hundreds of thousands of dollars, and some even spent millions. The unequal financial conditions and the illegitimate expenditures were the subject of many complaints on behalf of the 'poor' candidates to the CEC. In general, the CEC did not respond to these complaints, although exceptions were made in several cases when this would be to the advantage of the ruling power.

8. Voting

Voter Turn-out

It was a cold day on 7 November. Voter turn-out was low, and there was no incentive for the ruling power to exaggerate the figures too highly across the country. It was announced officially that 46.4% of voters took part in the elections. The opposition did not call this figure into question, even though, in some constituencies (particularly in the provinces), there was a mass practice of throwing ballots into the boxes in favour of the candidates of the ruling powers, which had a serious impact on the results. The quorum requirement was annulled by law, exit poll were carried out, and this time those in power did not oblige the local election commissions by artificially raising turn-out figures within the data of the territorial election commissions.

Utilising the Army and Other Institutions

In constituencies where leaders of the Azadlyg bloc were running, the ruling powers applied some well-tried tricks: soldiers and officers of the national army (stationed in the territory of the 36 Khatai), along with the 4th territorial election committee, all voted for the candidate of the ruling powers, Samed Seidov, competitor of Rasul Guliev,. Although Guliev was leading in all the territorial election commissions where civilians voted, the CEC annulled the results of several territorial election committees where he had a significant advantage. Samed Seidov won, with the votes of the soldiers and inmates of the women's penitentiary.

Against the Musavat leader Isa Gambar, those in power nominated a police officer, even though this practice is formally prohibited. Adil Aliev, brother of the head of the senior police department of Baku, Lieutenant-General Maharram Aliev, mobilised thousands of policemen and security staff, openly distributing money to voters, and 'won' over one of the most famous politicians in the country.[5] The many complaints by Isa Gambar's team on the obvious le-

---

5   *Yeni Musavat* and *Gundelic Azerbaijan*. 7 November 2005, with reference to information from Turan New Agency.

gal violations were ignored. As with other 'undesirable' winners, the CEC had a simple solution: the results of the elections were annulled, either in general in the territory, or in selected polling stations, thus determining the results of the whole territorial election commission.

Falsification of Results

The active opposition (Sardar Jalaloglu, Rovshan Veliev, Flora Kerimova and Arif Gadjyly), who had the final minutes of the territorial election commissions in their hands, were deprived of the victory by a decision of the CEC. Moreover, the heads of the executive power in Sumgait, Sabirabad and Zakataly (where Flora Kerimova, Panah Huseynov, and Arif Gadjyly had won clear victories) were dismissed from their positions for not being able to falsify the elections adequately. Rasul Guliev and Eldar Namazov were deprived of the victory through annulment of the results at several polling stations, and also due to the fact that the ruling power recorded 100% voter turn-out among the military and convicts. In the 29th Sabael constituency of Baku, the candidate for the Azadlyg bloc, Gasan Kerimov, won in all 29 polling stations where the residents of this constituency voted. In three polling stations, votes were cast by convicts of Bailovo prison in Baku, as well as a military hospital and a military detachment. A 26-year-old activist of the ruling party, Fuad Muradov, 'won' with an absolute result, and the CEC promptly issued a mandate for this young person to become a deputy.

The Reaction of the Opposition

After the results of the voting were announced, the opposition once again started to convene protest meetings. A gathering on 26 November was dispersed with exceptional brutality, and people were seriously wounded. After this, the opposition tried once again to organise a meeting in the centre of the city, but also this meeting was broken up. The constitutional court, having considered the CEC Minutes, annulled the results of the elections in six constituencies (in addition to the CEC ones), and approved the final results of the elections.

9. Conclusions

The 2005 parliamentary elections in Azerbaijan resulted in yet another victory of the state over society. In general, the democratic countries and organisations of the West recognised the results of the elections, though serious comments were voiced concerning the legal violations. As always, Russia, Iran and Turkey gave a positive assessment of the 'democratic' nature of the elections. The Parliamentary Assembly of the Council of Europe has continued its assessment work on the results of the elections: their final verdict will be issued after 13 May, when re-elections will be conducted in 10 constituencies.

Ten candidates from the opposition were elected into the parliament – ten whom those in power deemed to be conservative and 'constructive'. Those considered to be 'destructive' were not allowed into the parliament, despite the verdict from the electorate. Fifteen women were elected, which is two more than in the previous composition. From the ruling party Yeni Azerbaijan, 57 deputies were elected; four were elected from the opposition party Musavat. Since the elected 'independent' deputies can also be expected to support those in power, we may conclude that the performance, under the name of 'elections', was engineered to give the appearance of democracy, and to enable the ruling Aliev family to retain an absolute control over all institutions of state power.

Complaints were filed with the CEC by 82 candidates. CAC observers succeeded in getting 736 copies of minutes and the registration of 1,945 acts of election violations. The CAC has documentary confirmation of the victory of 25 candidates from the opposition and independents. However, few of these individuals will apply to the European Court of Human Rights. The citizens' belief in objectivity, and the efficacy of Western democracy, has been weakened.

For the first time since 1991, the national democratic press openly accused the USA of betraying the ideals of democracy, following double standards and collusion with the corrupt Aliev regime. Until November 2005, the norm for this press had been criticism of Russia and Iran, while the USA was criticised only by the Islamic press. Apparently the leaders of the national democrats had realised the futility of their hopes of gaining the powerful support of Washington. It allowed its own, rather controlled newspapers to divert public discontent away from themselves and onto the US ambassador, the US State Department, and President G.W. Bush.

The voting bloc 'YES' quickly disintegrated after the elections. Of all its candidates, only Eldar Namazov has continued the political struggle for getting the election results revised; he intends to challenge the decision of the constituency commission in the European Court. The Social-Democratic party intends to participate in the re-elections. The Azadlyg bloc is being torn apart by internal factions: the issue of whether to participate in the repeat elections in the ten constituencies on 13 May 2006 split the bloc. Musavat, which already has six deputies in the parliament, decided to participate, while the People's Front Party (PFP) and the Democratic Party, who gained no deputies in the elections, insist on a boycott. Such a difference of opinion is evidence of the Musavat understanding of the inevitability of the evolutionary development of the country, and the benefit of participating in the legitimate structures of the state. The position of the PFP, and of the Democratic Party, tells us about the determination to continue to make an attempt at an 'orange revolution'.

Once again, those in power have tried to cleanse the opposition field. The four Constitutional Courts annulled the decision of the CEC (on the approval of the mandates of two deputies from the PEP, Ali Kerimov and Gulangusein Alibeily) and left this party outside the parliament. After this, the deputy Sabir Rustanhanly (chair of the Civil Solidarity Party), apparently acting upon the instruction of the authorities to nominate the candidature of Enver Aliev as a representative of his own party to the CEC, repeatedly ran, in order to gain admission to this body. Enver Aliev stated that this was done in order to seek revenge for his having refused to sign the final minutes of the CEC. However, Vidadi Mahmudlu, Musavat representative in the CEC, did sign the final minutes of the falsified elections, thereby unleashing a storm of criticism against himself. Journalists of the opposition press started to discuss the size of the bribes he had received from the ruling power for the party shuffling.

The split in the National Independence party can be attributed to the results of the elections. The 'leader' of the party, Etibar Mamedov, started a struggle to the death with the chairperson of the Ali Aliev party. This chairperson tied

NIPA to the Azadlyg bloc, where the age-old competitor of Etibar Mamedov, Isa Gambar, runs the show. It resulted in the decision to convene two congresses of the same party – repeating the situation of five years earlier with the PFP, when the party split into 'reformers' and 'classics'. Also the Democratic Party could not avoid a split. A scandal flared up between the general secretary, Sardar Jalaloglu, and Aidyn Guliev, editor-in-chief of *Baki Xeber* (which is sponsored by the chairperson of the party, Rasul Guliev).

Dismay and embarrassment now reign in post-election Azerbaijan. However, braver and stronger-sounding voices calling for the establishment of a new political force may assess the status of society more soberly and deeply. It is to be hoped that they will be able to carry out a more rational and successful policy, putting an end to the systematic crisis into which the Aliev family has plunged the country. There is not much time left until 2008, when the next presidential elections are to be held.

V THE POST-ELECTION SITUATION: WHO RULES AZERBAIJAN?

Rustam Seyidov

1. Introduction

At first glance, there are no significant changes in Azerbaijan: the same group of people are in power. They were brought into the country's leadership by Heidar Aliev, the deceased president. Yet, even though Heidar Aliev's son took over from his father to become President (and, as he himself claims, in essence continues the policies of his father), we can note several changes. These changes are not related to policy directions, or to the social and economic measures taken, but are – significantly – found in the area involving the reallocation of authority.

Let us begin with a brief, retrospective look at the years which led to the existing situation. Without considering recent history, it is difficult to understand the current situation.

2. The State System under Heidar Aliev

Ideology

In 1993, after numerous dramatic events, Heidar Aliev, a KGB general and former member of the CPSU Politburo, became the President of Azerbaijan. He was a man with great intellectual potential, will, experience and firmness of purpose, and he started to build a system of power in the way he best understood. Along with all his undoubted personal merits, there was one more quality at the core of his ideology, and with this he led the country to its current status: in fact, Heidar Aliev hated Azerbaijanis, and viewed Azerbaijan through the prism of this hatred.

This can explain why, for many years, Azerbaijan ranked among the five most corrupt countries in the world. Why the Karabakh problem has not taken even a single step towards resolution since the ceasefire in 1994. Why health care, education, social protection, as well as other sectors, are in a catastrophic state, despite the country's huge oil and other natural resources.

Close Personal Ties

A key factor in the power system built by Heidar Aliev was the selection of managers based on close-knit local and family ties. This system of state-machinery building was certainly not original: it was based on the example of such African states as Nigeria, Senegal and Mali. Most state officials – from the prime minister and the head of the president's administration, to the police chiefs in remote areas of the country – come from either the Nakhichevan enclave within Azerbaijan or from Armenia, where, until the recent notorious events, hundreds of thousands of Azerbaijanis lived. Many of the president's relatives have obtained positions of responsibility and deputy mandates.[1] Furthermore, other officials often act in the same manner. Present-day Azerbaijan is managed by a 'family-parochial clan', or the FPC for short.

Preservation of Power

The ruling power had reached a *modus vivendi*, and it did everything possible to preserve it. During the first phase of his rule, Heidar Aliev physically and/or politically exterminated all bright political opponents who might act as if they

---

1   The brother of the former President (and thus the uncle of the current president), Jalal Aliev, became a deputy for the third time in a row. Likewise, Vasif Talybov, the head of Nakhychvan Autonomous Republic and the husband of Heidar Aliev's niece, was elected for the third time. Within 8 years, Beilyar Eyubov, who is married to another one of Heidar Aliev's nieces, who was previously a fire brigade foreman, became lieutenant-general, the chief of personal security and a very richt and influential person. The wife of Ilham Aliev, Mekhriban Alieva, became an MP. The uncle of the first lady is Azerbaijan ambassador to the USA, and another uncle was appointed Minister of Health to replace the recently arrested Ali Insanov. These are just the top state posts: the same thing occurs in business, entire sectors and spheres of which are controlled by members of the president's family.

had power, or who disagreed with his actions. These included Suret Gusei-nov, Ali Antsukhskyi, Gadji Vagif, Afiyatdin Jalilov, Rasul Guliev and others. Perhaps oddly, this list did not include leaders of the national and democratic opposition, given the entirely irreconcilable struggle between this section of the opposition and the ruling party, but this will be discussed later.

All key posts in the state were allocated to rather faceless individuals from the FPC system, notable for their personal loyalty to the president. The peo-ple were managed under a system of permitted and privately encouraged cor-ruption; and through these people, the state was in turn managed (for exam-ple, by paying extremely low wages to the staff of the budgetary organisations and structures). According to some former members of the deceased presi-dent's team, discrediting information was collected on all the ministers, and this was also practised down the vertical line of command. Very quickly this became the norm for the functioning of all state organisations and large busi-nesses, which were headed by large state figures and members of the FPC. It became clear that if a large share of the corrupt money and various bribes were transferred to the higher levels of power, the law would be deaf and blind to it. Corruption, and hence, the presence of discrediting information, was a major lever of the FPC management system. This vertical line was headed by the President himself, who was widely acknowledged as a person with a multi-billion fortune. Under such conditions, it was only natural that the ruling FPC became a solid organisation, absolutely obedient to the iron will of its founder and leader. Due to the absence of real opposition, the system worked smoothly – at least until Heidar Aliev's serious illness and death.

3. Transfer of Power to the Son

During the period involving Heidar Aliev's health problems, his trips to the USA for treatment, and then his coronary operation, society sustained rumours about the possibility of the elderly President transferring power to his son. However, it seems that, in reality, Heidar Aliev did not even think of transferring power to his son; he clearly realised his son's capabilities – i.e. that his son had an aversion to politics. Furthermore, he recognised the wolf-like nature of the FPC members who were managing Azerbaijan. However, with the onset of his illness, he may have been the one heating up these rumours; certain amendments had even been introduced to the Constitution, whereby the person who replaced the President was to be the prime minister (but not the Speaker of the Parliament). Since the prime minister was a rather faceless person, this was accepted by society. More importantly, it was taken by the Establishment as a clear sign that the president's son, Ilham Aliev, would become prime minister in the near future. All these measures had been taken by the President in order to calm down FPC members, to reassure them that 'even if the father passes away, the son will arrive and nothing will have changed in the state machine'. However, in reality, throughout all years of Heidar Aliev's rule, his son had occupied the post of the Vice-President of the state oil company, turning up at his office only intermittently. This is no secret in the city, as everyone can witness at what time the motorcade of the president's son (now the president) leaves for his office and the roads are blocked for this procession. Even after the amendments to the Constitution, when the whole society expected Ilham Aliev to be appointed prime minister, this did not happen. This appointment would have been a clear sign that Heidar Aliev wished to see his son in his post; however important his son's position in the oil company might be, the post of the prime minister is one a very different scale of power and responsibility. Undoubtedly, Heidar Aliev understood this, and had he really wished to see his son as president, he would have appointed Ilham Aliev as prime minister under him, to acquire the experience necessary to be able to manage the country.

Supposedly, the President did eventually sign the decree which appointed Ilham Aliev as prime minister. However, the point at which this is theoretically said to have occurred fully contradicts common sense, i.e. at a time just before his death, when he was already in a clinic in Turkey, and when all Azerbaijan was sure that even if he was not about to die, he was certainly unconscious and incapable of acting sensibly. It seems that this decree had been inspired by the top of the FPC, with the collusion of the international public. The FPC needed Ilham Aliev to support them and prevent the possibility of a loss of power and money in circumstances of significant political changes in the country. It is evident that Ilham Aliev, who is well-known in many casinos around the world, faced such ultimatums more than once, and that he could not reject them. He agreed to become prime minister, with the clear understanding that this would inevitably lead to his appointment as President in the near future.

4. The 2003 Presidential Elections

Ilham Aliev: the New President

The 'presidential elections' in 2003 could have had no other outcome than the announcement of Ilham Aliev as president. After the death of Heidar Aliev, there were great hopes for serious changes (if not reforms), aimed at the laws which regulated life in society. However, more reflective observers realised that these hopes would never come true. Firstly, there was (and still is) no real opposition to the FPC rule. In addition came another serious factor which had helped the FPC to push Ilham Aliev into the presidency: the position of the Western community. Azerbaijani society firmly believes that Heidar Aliev died in Turkey, and that his body was taken to the USA and was kept there for some months. Whether or not this is true, there is no doubt that the fatally ill President was incapable of acting, in Turkey or in the USA. He never made any statements on TV or radio, or gave telephone interviews. This seems odd, as Heidar Aliev knew well the potential influence of television on the formation of the public opinion. Prior to his illness, he had used it skilfully, sometimes even excessively: not a single day passed without his lengthy speeches on TV.

The Position of the West

This state of affairs was a clear indication that the USA (and, eventually, the whole Western community) was in fact satisfied with FPC rule. It is impossible to prove that the FPC received real political support from the West (by that time, the ruling elite did not need money), but the collusion, indifference and passive support to the FPC was clearly understood by the most powerful players. The FPC practically decided that it had been given *carte blanche* for total falsification of the elections and shameless violation of the laws. The presidential elections ended in bloodshed: hundreds of protestors wounded and at least one demonstrator officially recognised as having been killed by the police (although human rights organisations stated that the figure was far higher). Western interest in the ruling clan was confirmed by numerous statements of various international bodies, declaring the elections 'one more step on the path to democracy'. No less numerous were the congratulations to 'newly elected' President Ilham Aliev from the heads of the states and governments of Western countries.

The situation during this presidential election, as during all the previous ones and the recent parliamentary elections as well, could have been completely different. The attitude of the world to events in Azerbaijan could have been different too, had it not been for Heidar Aliev's main achievement – that of safeguarding power in hands of the FPC.

5. The Opposition

The Popular Front of Azerbaijan (PFA)

In recent decades, the first political opposition party in Azerbaijan was the Popular Front of Azerbaijan (PFA). Its establishment and development is directly connected with the beginning of the Karabakh conflict. At that time, in 1988, Azerbaijan was still within the Soviet Union. Having started as a democratic organisation, the PFA quickly took on a national, democratic, and often populist and pan-Turkic nature. PFA chairman was former dissident Abulfaz Alchibey, who publicly declared his unlimited respect and admiration for Heidar Aliev. After only one year in power (June 1992–June 1993), Abulfaz Elchibey and his supporters came to grief and demonstrated their complete feebleness in managing the state. They started to call for Heidar Aliev (then in Nakhichevan) to take over power. After repeated requests, and after an aircraft had been dispatched to Nakhichevan, Heidar Aliev came to Baku. On the same day, President Abulfaz Aliev fled to his native village (also in Nakhichevan). The PFA gave birth to two more parties with a national-democratic orientation, Musavat and the Party of National Independence of Azerbaijan.

As of today, the largest and most structured oppositional parties in Azerbaijan, with branches throughout the country, are *Musavat* (led by Isa Gambar); the *Popular Front of Azerbaijan* party (led by Ali Kerimli); and the *Democratic Party of Azerbaijan* (led by Rasul Guliev). The Party of National Independence has lost its influence.

The Contradictory Nature of the 'Opposition'

Analysing the activities of the first two parties while Heidar Aliev and then his son were in power, we see that at all the key moments of development and potential change, the leaders of these parties adopted decisions which finally proved favourable for the ruling FPC. Many examples confirm this statement, but, since this article concerns a different subject, let us look at only one here – an instance that contributed to the weakening and split of the opposition. In

2000, prior to the parliamentary elections, the opposition keenly discussed the possibility of conducting elections with the help of the United Nations. Of course, the UN could have done so only with government approval, but the very fact of a unified opposition turning to the UN could have had a strong political influence on the pre-election situation, and indeed on the elections as well. Representatives of the opposition were dispatched to the USA, to deliver a letter signed by the leaders of all the major parties, as well as those of numerous 'virtual' [one-man] parties. When the envoys arrived at UN headquarters and proudly handed their letter to a high-level official, he reached for another letter on his table: this bore the signatures of the same people, signed one day later, and declared that the Azerbaijan opposition did not consider it necessary for the parliamentary elections to be conducted with the help of the UN.[2]

This example is only one of the many which prove that the opposition in Azerbaijan does not correspond to its purpose, but has a very important and serious mission defined for it by Heidar Aliev. This includes channelling moods of protest; expressing economic, social and political demands in a marginal form, which in turn causes rejection by much of society; and, finally, dissipating the desire for the reforms during futile meetings which are suppressed with awesome brutality from time to time.

For this reason, confidence in these parties is steadily decreasing, while, on the other hand, another part of society has placed its hopes in these parties. The latter group uses the following reasoning: there is no other opposition, so the present opposition, although very bad, is still better than those in power today.

All elections in recent years have been repeated with a frightening consistency. It would seem that this is a vicious circle, with no end. Who can fight the regime, and how can they fight it, if the political opposition is secretly cooperates with and getting financial support from those against whom it is supposed to be struggling? However, we may note one interesting phenomenon which could change the state of affairs radically – the case of Rasul Guliev.

---

2   This story is related in full in "Real Azerbaijan" (Realniy Azerbaijan) № 5, 13 May 2005 (the article by Z. Alizade, 'A Request to the UN', can be found at: www.realazer.com).

Rasul Guliev

A Genuine Threat
Rasul Guliev, an ex-Speaker of the parliament and previously close party as-
sociate, has become a very dangerous competitor to the Aliev clan within the
FPC in the struggle for power. Considerable activity has focused on trying to
enable his return to Baku. From the period beginning with Heidar Aliev coming to power, to Rasul Guliev's forced retirement from the post of parliamentary Speaker and ensuing emigration to the West in 1996, Rasul Guliev became the most powerful man, after Heidar Aliev, in the ruling FPC. This also
refers to his financial opportunities and to his weight in the ruling power elite.
Like most members of the FPC, Rasul Guliev is a native of Nakhichevan.

A Disgraced but Inseparable Agent
On 23 April, 2005, the magazine *Khesabat* published a list of the 30 richest
people in Azerbaijan. Here we mention only the first ten, with their positions:

- Kamaladdin Heidarov, chairman of the State Customs Committee;
- Jamal Aliev, Deputy (and the President's uncle);
- Ramil Usubov, Minister of the Interior;
- Ali Insanov, Minister of Health (arrested on 18 October 2005; the first
  lady's uncle was appointed to this post);
- Paolo Parviz, Turkish businessman;
- Beilyar Ajubov, head of presidential security;
- Heidar Babaev, chairman of the State Commission on Securities (and
  current Minister of Economic Development, replacing Farhad Aliev,
  who has been arrested);
- Ziya Mamedov, Minister of Transport;
- Misir Mardanov, Minister of Education;
- Elman Rustamov, chairman of the board of the National Bank.

Of these ten, Paolo Parviz does not occupy a public post. Only Ramil
Usubov, Ziya Mamedov and Paolo Parviz (who is Turkish) do not come from

Nakhichevan or Armenia; and almost the same proportion are representatives of the natives of one particular area –a characteristic not only of the remaining twenty people, but of the whole system of power, from the top of the vertical chain of command, down to the bottom. Those few ministers from other regions try to copy the general method of recruitment of staff and trustees. For instance, in the area surrounding Ramil Usubovwho is a native of Karabakh, his landsmen prevail. The Minister of Defence appointed a 30-year old colonel, his close relative, as a corps commandant, at a time when the Azerbaijani army consisted of only three corps. This is a strong system of false and obstinate paternalism, whereby power and money are received from higher officers due to their connections and/or parochial relationships (rather than based on knowledge and competence): the rules of solidarity and cohesion are supreme, rather than the law. This system is one reason why Rasul Guliev was seen as an inseparable ingredient, despite being a disgraced member of the FPC.

The Return of Rasul Guliev

A Change of Circumstance
When Heidar Aliev was alive and healthy, numerous promises were made concerning Rasul Guliev's return to Azerbaijan. These were not taken seriously by society or within the FPC itself. However, since the death of Heidar Aliev, the situation changed for the worse, and with a weak new President, Ilham Aliev, these statements began to be taken more seriously.

Initially, statements about the return of Rasul Guliev were made, once more, prior to the presidential elections. However, these were not a all realistic, not least because Guliev was not yet in the plans of the USA concerning Azerbaijan. Yet with the arrival of 2005, once again statements appeared concerning the forthcoming return of Rasul Guliev to his motherland. Moreover, unlike all previous parliamentary and presidential elections, this time his candidacy for parliament was officially approved by the Central Election Commission. The return of Rasul Guliev had become quite a realistic proposition. Within society and the ruling elite, there was a clear understanding that this would mean an inevitable withdrawal (whether this be slow, or even delayed) of the current team from power. This is not anticipated for reason of his public support, but is rather because he was one of those who ruled the country together with the FPC. It must be remembered that the radical political changes in Ukraine and Georgia were possible only when the heads of the opposition were also part of the commanding elite. The Kuchma regime in Ukraine, and the Shevardnadze regime in Georgia, had been causing hostility, or possibly even hatred, within the people for a long period. However, the regime changed only after the split occurred within the ruling group. Heidar Aliev fully controlled his team and prevented any attempts for independence by any member of the FPC. We cannot say the same about Ilham Aliev, who has appeared rather indifferent to his presidential duties.

There appeared to be some disorder, and fight for influence, among the various high-level officials of the FPC (each of whom has unlimited financial opportunities). One outcome of such disorder was the retirement of Namik Abbasov, Minister of National Security Throughout his life, Namik Abbasov served in the security bodies of the Soviet Union. Prior to his being offered the post of Deputy Minister of National Security in Baku, by Abulfaz Elchibey, he had served as Deputy Head of the Murmansk Department of the KGB of the USSR. He became a minister during the period when Heidar Aliev came to power, and was one of the closest and most faithful workers of the president. He was later dismissed, and Eldar Mahmudov, Colonel of Militia, has since replaced him. However, during his term in office, the level of corruption within the ministry became comparable with that of the police – one of the most corrupt state power structures in the entire system.

Preparing for Battle
Nevertheless, Rasul Guliev's possible return threatened the ruling clan so much that, on the day of his announced arrival, Baku was reminiscent of a city under siege. Thousands of policemen and soldiers of the internal troops were wearing battle attire and were accompanied by dogs. They blocked the airport and its connecting roads. Guliev was prevented from arriving in Baku, and within a day several ministers and other high-ranking officials were arrested.

Why did the possibility of Rasul Guliev's return become so realistic in these elections, when it had been so unrealistic in the parliamentary elections of 2000, and the presidential elections of 2003? In telephone conversations with functionaries in his party, Guliev kept making assurances that he would be registered, that the Ministry of Internal Affairs of Azerbaijan would resolve the documentation problems, and that he would come to Baku for certain. For this reason, it is assumed that, in respect of his arrival, strong pressure was exerted on the authorities of Azerbaijan. This assumption is supported by the fact that it was during the pre-election period when an agreement was reached over the construction two US radar stations: one on the border with Iran, and another on the border with Russia.[3] Was this the cost for prohibiting the return of Guliev?

Arrests

All the arrested individuals were found guilty of attempting to start a revolution and of having secret relations with Rasul Guliev. Considering the disorder in the ruling team, such an explanation sounds rather logical: even when Heidar Aliev was alive, a part of the ruling elite tended to side with the former Speaker of Parliament (sometimes secretly and sometimes openly). For instance, after the old President suffered his first stroke in 2000, several deputies from the ruling party defiantly quit the party and became members of Rasul Guliev's party. Thus, expectations relating to Guliev's political reanimation were always high, both in society and in the ruling FPC itself.

However, it would be naive to relate the wide wave of arrests of high-ranking officials to the expected return of Rasul Guliev alone. It may well have been simply good power-sharing practice. The fight that occurred between one of the most powerful individuals, Kamalddin Heidarov (chairman of the State Customs Committee) and Farhad Aliev (Minister of Economic Development, later arrested), appeared in the opposition press as much as a year to a year and half before the election campaign. Dismissals and arrests have

---

3   Information on the construction of radar stations caused interest and was widely discussed in the press. The US Embassy in Baku confirmed this information, with reference to the Ambassador, while press secretary of the Ministry of Defence Ramiz Melikov refused to confirm or deny it. For example, there was an article in the Baku Russian-language newspaper, *Nezavisimaya Gazeta,* of 30 September 2005, titled 'Leakage of particular importance', written by Elshan Abulfatov. By 8 December, the Russian newspaper *Krasnaya Zvezda* cited Rino Harnish, US Ambassador in Azerbaijan, as saying that the future radar stations would be called to oversee the water space of the Caspian Sea.

continued, but are no longer passed off as 'attempts at revolution'. On the other hand, it is also difficult to explain these arrests by the fact that the President wishes to renew the team and hold some reforms. It looks more like a re-allocation of the powerful authorities within the FPC. The results of elections, at any level, in 'Aliev' Azerbaijan may be considered as an appointment and an expression of confidence by the FPC, and vice versa. Conversely, when an individual is prohibited from taking up an elected post, this is considered to be a demonstration of discontent, at best.

6. The Recent Elections

Current Parliamentary Composition

The average observer may feel some hope when looking through the list. Besides the ruling party, 13 political parties and blocs are represented in the parliament, most of whom declare their opposition. Here we shall not discuss the suitability of these circumstances, but will just review some of their results. From the ruling party, 57 candidates gained seats in the parliament, and an additional 40 have positioned themselves as independent deputies. There is no doubt about these 40 individuals: all are promoted by the FPC and have received their mandates with FPC consent. There are also several deputies who, despite declaring their political independence, provide comprehensive and consistent support to any action taken by the FPC. Finally, there are about 10 deputies who, to varying degrees, may be considered as 'representatives of the opposition', but who, as mentioned, secretly work in close co-operation with the FPC.

Points of Interest

It is interesting to note that 53 deputies from the ruling party got into the parliament twice, while four former deputies and members of the Higher Political Council (of the ruling party) failed to renew their mandates. In the previous parliament, representatives of the ruling party prevailed. However, in practice, 'independent' deputies are rather predictable and manageable, so the number of deputies nominated by the ruling party can be reduced. Even more interestingly, Zelimkhan Yagub, Seid Aran, Sattar Safarov and Zakhid Garalov all failed to gain seats. Each of these individuals has close parochial relations and an affinity with the ruling elite, and there has been no reason to doubt their loyalty. Moreover, Zelimkhan Yagub and Seid Aran provided perfect examples for the ideological framework of the 'Yeni Azerbaijan' party: their faces were constantly visible, on television and in the press, and would have been considered very helpful in case of public discontent involving the FPC. However, whilst most deputies appear in the parliament again and again, this quad seems to have lost out in the elections. This case fits the hypothesis about the processes of disorder and the reallocation of power in the FPC perfectly.

Also notable is the fact that one of the country's most famous writers, Anar Rzaev, lost out in the 'elections'. One of the components of Heidar Aliev's policy was 'feeding' and providing various privileges to the high status intelligentsia, as well as more generally to anyone somehow popular in society, such as people from the arts and mass culture – who, in return, were expected to remain uncritical of those in power. Rzaev had won a parliamentary seat in the last two elections. However, this time he failed, because, several years ago, he disagreed with the obstruction of Rasul Guliev and left the chamber when this issue was discussed. Although he remained silent for the next 10 years, and he occasionally advocated and actively protected the current regime, this did not help him. The leader of the clan, Heidar Aliev, used to figure issues out in advance and predict the political consequences of his actions. Today, without his leadership, the clan acts thoughtlessly and mercilessly.

Overview of the Recent Election Situation

Heidar Aliev accurately felt the need for a balance between the public trends and the predatory nature of the FPC. However, this has finally, and unalterably, been lost. After the FPC had realised that they had managed to prevent the return of Rasul Guliev, the worst-case scenario began to unfold. The practice of engineering the elections, as well as the forced suppression of those who held opposition views (not to be confused with the leaders of the pseudo-opposition national-democratic parties), was expanded to such a scale that even kind-hearted observers from many international organisations found it difficult to call the elections a 'step towards democracy'. Here we should remind the reader of the cruel crackdown on the peaceful meeting of 26 November. This meeting, which had been authorised by the authorities, had protested against the rigged elections. For the first time in recent history, women and children were cruelly beaten, and, allegedly, four people were killed.[4]There have been countless times when leaders of the national democratic opposition have directed protest as well as public hostility against the ruling regime, into pointless meetings. These always lead to cruel counter-action and thus invalidate society's hopes of a better future. Several hundred people participated in the meeting on 24 December 2005, which was declared and authorised by the ruling power. The election results were approved by the Constitutional Court and foolishly accepted by the Western community. Furthermore, political appearances were made by people who appeared in various forms, but yet obviously characterised the nature of power.

4   This can be read in statements made by the Steering Advisory Council 'For Free and Fair Election' (uniting more than 40 NGOs), at www.msim.az; in the newspapers *Azadlyg* No. 259, of 27 November, 2005; *Eni Musavat* No. 302, of 27 November 2005; and *Real Azerbaijan* No. 34, of 2 December 2005.

7. The Silent Speaker and the Criminal Authority

The Silence of the Parliamentary Speaker: Oktai Asadov

Until 1996, the Speaker of the Parliament was Rasul Guliev, who had also previously served as director of a huge oil refinery and then deputy prime minister of the country. On 16 October, 1996, Heidar Aliev chose to have Rasul Guliev replaced by Prof. Murtuz Aleskerov (head chair of state law at Azerbaijan State University). 'Elected' to be the Speaker of the new parliamentary assembly, was Oktai Asadov, who had run the country's water facilities (he headed the 'Azersu' association). Even though he has already served two terms in parliament, it is difficult to find much information about him. As the press has noted, in a rather mocking manner, for the past 10 years this man has held the record for being most reticent individual. He has neither brought, nor offered, any initiatives. He did not say a single word at all, not even when there was a request to switch on air-conditioners because of the sweltering heat, or when there was a request to keep the doors closed because of the draft.

The facelessness of the Speaker of the parliament indicates that he must be a transient, temporary figure. At present, this suits everybody, as the configuration of the ruling power in the post-election period has not yet been completely determined. In general, the appointment of Oktai Asadov means that no new person with extensive authority has appeared at the top level of the FPC. In the best-case scenario, the prime ministership (currently held by Arthur Rasizade, whose existence is frequently forgotten even by political scientists and experts) is being readied for him. A more pessimistic forecast is that Asadov will simply hold the position until a significantly stronger figure can be found.

The Criminal Element in the Parliament: Gusein Abdullaev

It is difficult to tell who the most authoritative figure might now be. However, one of the most interesting and significant results of the latest parliamentary elections was that Gusein Abdullaev (commonly known by the nickname

'Guska') succeeded in gaining a seat. This in itself indicates that the most au-thoritative figure must currently be found within criminal circles.

The Presence of Armed Groups

After Heidar Aliev came to power, the nickname 'Guska' became well known within general society. The rallies of 1998, 2000, 2003 and 2005 were broken up by a number of young people, notable for their exceptional cruelty, sparing neither known politicians nor women. Various prominent political figures re-ceived severe beatings, including Etibar Mamedov, Panah Huseynov, Lala Gadjieva and Iliyas Ismailov. Both the police and other power structures de-nied their involvement. Gradually rumours started spreading which suggested that the perpetrators belonged to the illegal armed groups of some ministers and businessmen.

Gusein Abdullaev's Armed Group

This author personally conversed with one man who served in Gusein Abdul-laev's group. Furthermore, in 1997, a member of the social-democratic party of Azerbaijan informed this writer that, in his region (Nakhichevan), jobless young men are offered the chance to move to Baku, where they get a good salary and a car. In return, they must keep an automatic weapon at home and, as required, act as protection for the authorities.[5] It is widely acknowledged that Gusein Abdullaev maintains an armed group at his own expense, num-bering somewhere between 500 to 800 men. This has now been openly writ-ten about in the mass media, and it is highly probable that this was done with Abdullaev's consent. It may be assumed that he is attempting to instil fear into people, and thereby strengthen his position. It is clear that one has to have the financial sources necessary in order to keep so many people, at relatively highly monthly salaries. Abdullaev also has a background in busi-ness. It is difficult to tell on what basis his business prospered, but at one of the meetings broadcast on TV, Heidar Aliev cited Gusein Abdullaev as pro-

---

5   In a country where political journalists are killed, they write very little and with great caution. However, it is impossible to hide everything completely. Attempts are even made at whitewashing people like Gusein Abdullaev – for example, the newspaper *Real Azerbaijan* ran an article about him which went over three issues, Nos. 35, 37 and 38 for 2005 (these articles can be found at www.realazer.com).

viding an example to his ministers. He may well be a highly successful businessman, but the existence of a big group armed with automatic weapons, as well as persistent rumours that he even holds a specific rank within gangster circles, suggest rather different reasons for his success in business and his strength within the system of state authority. Thus, for example, it is known (from informal sources and from information provided in some newspapers), that the head of the socio-political department of the president's administration, Ali Gasanov, worked as a weigher (weighing scrap metal in order for it to be exported from the country), and the present head of the state petroleum company (GNKAR), Rovnag Abdullaev (also the deputy of the newly elected parliament), was an assistant in one of Gusein Abdullaev's firms. Presumably, some ministers are also directly linked to this man.

Gusein Abdullaev: Sources of Power and Influence

It seems highly likely that all Gusein Abdullaev's power and influence is the result of the protection and support provided by Heidar Aliev. He needed such people and groups of *tonton-makuts* to suppress public discontent. Similar groups, with significantly smaller numbers, are kept by high-ranking members of the FPC. But Heidar Aliev understood well that, by admitting such people into the realm of public policy and allowing them to occupy state posts, he could potentially lose control of them, so they were permitted to act behind the scenes only. Gusein Abdullaev had never before dared to stand for parliament.

8. The Presidency of GNKAR

Rovnag Abdullaev: An Unlikely Candidate

From this point of view, the appointment of Rovnag Abdullaev, an engineer (actually a builder by trade), who had worked in the petroleum sector for only two years, as President of the GNKAR, seems interesting. Firstly, it is difficult to overestimate the importance of this post. The major share of the revenue of the country, as well as most 'corruption money', is provided by GNKAR. Oil, and everything else connected with extraction, processing, and infrastructure in the petroleum industry and petroleum mechanical engineering, is the backbone of the economy and the source of the real money in Azerbaijan. For example, almost 60% of the expenditure budget of Azerbaijan for 2006 is to be financed by the payment from foreign exchange receipts from oil sales.[6] It was for this reason that Ilham Aliev was nominated to the post of Vice-President of GNKAR.

Appointments under the Rule of Heidar Aliev

During the entire period of Heidar Aliev's government, the President of GNKAR was Natik Aliev, an oil-industry worker and experienced manager. Few could have predicted that such a key post would be occupied by a person who, only two years previously, had been the director of an oil refining factory and no longer dealt directly with oil. Nevertheless, Natik Aliev was dismissed from this position, and appointed as the Minister of Industry and Energy – a formal post, without any influence or power opportunities. There were also some re-arrangements in the presidential office: let us just say that the position as head of one of the key departments of the president's administration was occupied by an old buddy of the president.

The parliamentary elections marked the starting point of the changes in the configuration of authority. There have been a lot of changes, and they will undoubtedly continue. However, the essential part of the authority will not be

---

6   *Zerkalo*, 12 January 2005.

touched, because that still rests with the FPC. Heidar Aliev, a skilled politician and the founder of the pyramid of power, has left this world. Now another group of people, formally led by Ilham Aliev, are trying to keep the power. Time will show whether they succeed, but today the most powerful figures in the power structure are two individuals: Ramiz Mehtiev and Kamaladdin Heidarov.

9. Ramiz Mehtiev and Kamaladdin Heidarov

The New Driving Force

The general opinion after Heidar Aliev's death was that the main driving force in the pyramid of power was the head of the presidential administration (widely known as a 'power broker'), Ramiz Mehtiev. Also Kamaladdin Heidarov started growing stronger during the pre-election period. After Ilham Aliev was 'elected' president, there were many replacements of heads of administrations in various regions. It seems clear that a major part of the deputies in the parliament are the protégés of one or the other of these two individuals. R. Mehtiev will gain power in fulfilling the overall tasks of governing the republic, quite often substituting the president. K. Heidarov gains his power from the fact that he is not only one of the richest people in Azerbaijan, but he also controls its main financial flows. It is notable that the Minister of Taxes, the chairman of the social protection fund, as well as various other high-ranking officials, had all previously served in various posts of the Customs Committee. Moreover, society openly discussed how much Kamaladdin Heidarov paid for getting his people into various posts, a figure which ran into millions of dollars.

The FPC: Stagnation and Degeneration

The parliamentary elections have shown that the FPC is set to continue the policy of Heidar Aliev. Yet, now that he is gone, this policy becomes grotesque, with obvious attributes of stagnation and rapid degeneration. Ilham Aliev announced a policy of resolutely fighting against corruption, but he then appointed Ramiz Mehtiev, one of the founders of the corrupt national system, to chair the State Commission on Anti-Corruption. In his turn, Kamaladdin Heidarov is also becoming one of the most influential figures, even though bribes are already being accepted in his own department. These bribes are taken only in the presence of witnesses: this practice is used to avoid any doubts about the size of the bribes taken, and is transmitted upwards through the vertical system of the officials. What will be the outcome of this power de-generation in Azerbaijan?

10. Impact of External Forces: Probable Outcomes

A Determining Factor

The impact of external forces on the country becomes a crucial factor in such conditions. Earlier in this article, we discussed the bargaining likely to have taken place between the ruling power and the USA, whereby the price of the positive reforms (which only R. Guliev could currently fulfil) were two radar stations. However, there is another indicative example. Almost immediately after the appointment of Rovnag Abdullaev as GNKAR president, British Petroleum announced a sharp increase in oil output expected for 2006. In connection with the oil strategy and its impact on the authorities in Azerbaijan, we should note that the resignation and arrest of Farhad Aliev were accompanied by the arrest of his brother (President of Azpetrol, the largest oil-trading company in Azerbaijan), as well as the resignation of the President of the company Azertrans (included in the Azpetrol holding), which transported oil by tankers from Central Asia to terminals in Baku, and then by rail to Batumi and further to global markets. In light of these facts, the story surrounding Farhad Aliev and the rearrangements made to the fuel and energy arrangements acquire somewhat different meanings.

Forces of Influence in Azerbaijan

We may distinguish among three differently directed forces of influence in Azerbaijan:

- First, the USA and, in many respects, the other Western countries. The USA and the European countries are anxious about international terrorism, as well as about controlling petroleum flows. This lead them to give their support to FPC as the party in power. This then robs the people and disorganises the country, instead of supporting and helping democratic trends in its development.
- Secondly, Russia, due to the misguided views it holds about its greatness and power. Russia wants to keep its influence in Azerbai-

jan, and it too finds that the best way to reach this goal is to help the ruling FPC.

- Thirdly, Iran, where the theocrats in power dream of expanding their religious beliefs throughout the world. However, Azerbaijan is a deeply secular country. It would appear impossible for an Islamic renaissance to occur here, although in recent decades the number of believers has increased significantly.

Azerbaijan and Islam

'Spiritual Department of the Caucasian Muslims'
In this connection, we should recall that the policy which the ruling power conducts towards religion is similar to the policy it conducts towards the opposition. During the Soviet era, there emerged a rather strange organisation named 'Spiritual Department of the Caucasian Muslims' – strange for two reasons:

- Firstly, such an organisation cannot exist if one proceeds from the norms, canons, instructions and rules of Islam. The communities of believers were independent and initially the organisation had no vertical line of power: consequently, it contradicted Islam.
- Secondly, one might think that this organisation existed as one of the forms of control over believers carried out by retaliatory bodies of the Soviet Union. However, 15 years have passed since Azerbaijan gained its independence, yet this organisation continues to exist and prosper, together with its permanent leader from the Soviet period, Allhshukyur Pashadze, often jokingly (?) referred to as a KGB colonel. It is difficult to make a judgement about this, but he certainly he enjoys the full support of the circles of power and was even forgiven by them. He has declared himself the lifelong leader of his department.

The Youth of Azerbaijan and Islam
There is also is another part of Islam, connected to the fact that there are a growing number of young people desperate to find fulfilment in their lives.

This desperation is caused by many reasons, of varying triviality: university fees, general bribery in the education system, the strict social class system. These young people turn to religion for support and internal peace of mind. Both Iran and various Arab countries are actively working in this direction, and are especially active in the southern regions of Azerbaijan. The discontented and anxious lives of young people push them towards actions of protest and it is here, once again, that they are helped by religious organisations and mosques of the *vahhabit* type.

Current Position

For the time being, these organisations are not particularly strong, and thus the state generally prefers not to take notice of them. The ruling clan sees Allhshukyur Pashadze (who is entrenched in the system of corruption, and maintains various relationships within governmental circles) as the most convenient tool for governing that most complex of social phenomenon, the religious sentiments of people. The power structures are also used to supporting him: in 2004, police forces surrounded the Djuma mosque, whose imam of which was Ilgar. Believers were not allowed to enter. The logic of the authorities was clear. This mosque had previously attracted many intelligent and cultural people with scientific degrees. Ilgar is himself a graduate in philosophy and a highly educated theologian. Understandably, he is not liked by the authorities After the presidential elections in 2003, he was also arrested, to be released only several months later. People unified by one idea (whether political doctrine or religious belief) are undesirable, and even dangerous, for the authorities. However, the processes caused by the power elite itself cannot be easily stopped either.

11. Conclusion

Azerbaijan is ruled by the same parochial family clan that was brought to power by Heidar Aliev. Continuation of the clan's power will result in the degeneration of society as a whole. If this occurs, then any options are possible – not excluding the serious influence and dangerous strengthening of fundamentalist Islam. It is natural that the structures of civil society (which are gradually developing in the country) try to resist the negative tendencies leading to the degradation of the people and the state. Yet it is difficult to speak of any real success when we realise that democratically minded persons and the political and non-governmental organisations alike have to resist not only internal opponents, but also the surrounding world. It would be far more difficult for the ruling clan to maintain power if this, for whatever reason, was seen as unsuitable for the West and Russia, and Iran, and even Armenia.

VI ECONOMIC IMPLICATIONS OF THE PARLIA-MENTARY ELECTIONS: SYMBIOSIS OF POLITICS AND ECONOMICS

Torgrul Juvarly & Ali Abasov

1. Introduction

Forecasting the Future

'A politician thinks about the next elections, a statesman – about future generations'

Today it is generally recognised that Azerbaijan must undergo comprehensive reforms, or else future generations will face far more serious problems. Sadly, the most recent set of elections, and the consequent situation, have shown that Azerbaijan has plenty of politicians, but few statesmen. Suffice it to refer to statements made by leading politicians regarding the outlook for Azerbaijan: it is difficult to see even medium-term forecasts. Over the next 8 to 10 years, Azerbaijan will rapidly be getting richer – to be followed by an equally rapid fall in oil revenues. If, by the end of this period, the country does not manage to carry out a programme of reforms, and it does not reach a level of efficient export production, then it might well enter a period of chronic economic crisis. Azerbaijan has quite a limited period of time – roughly the next 10 years – in which to find a way to mobilise all its resources, so as to minimise future challenges and threats. Initially, this involves breaking out of the rather large list of countries that are classified as 'lagging behind'.

The November Elections: an Economic Perspective

Capital
Strange as it may seem, the role of capital (particularly national capital) in the political processes in Azerbaijan has yet to be sufficiently studied. Everyone knows (or suspects) that it is capital that gives the political structure its systemic nature, and that capital is also the reason why this structure prefers to act predominantly behind the scenes. Such processes are frequently repeated in many CIS countries, but the peculiarities lie in the differences – in the pace of the institutional reforms, in the barriers to business, and in the gradual reduction of the level of corruption

Failure to Create a Competitive Environment
This article does not analyse the purely political implications of the November parliamentary elections: our focus is on aspects directly related to economics. Let us first take note of only one central political and economic outcome of the most recent elections: once again, the aim of creating of a competitive political environment has failed, thereby jeopardising the opportunities for creating a setting conducive to economic competition in the post-election period.

Symbiosis of Politics and Economy
We argue that there is a symbiosis of politics and economy in Azerbaijan. Here it is essential to understand the interaction between the expanding private sector and the state-controlled part of the economy. The state-controlled section is still considerable: the state has visible levers of administrative influence, which it uses actively in order to solidify its monopoly positions. As long as this type of relation prevails, normal progress towards a market economy will meet artificial barriers. Indeed, the country's market economy is starting to resemble a mere imitation, just like its democracy.

Discussions and Assessments

In the following we discuss the economic basis of the latest elections, as well as the current economic situation. We consider the strategies of economic development in Azerbaijan as compared with some CIS countries, and analyse some of the governmental institutions that regulate the Azerbaijani economy. It will be important to assess the degree of their transparency of these institutions, their independence and their relations to political groups. What we seek to do is to investigate the degree to which government institutions are able to rationally regulate the economy. Finally, we present possible formats for changes to the existing system, in the context of future scenarios for Azerbaijan.

2. The Starting Point for Azerbaijan

Oil and Developing Countries

A Fight for Control
In those developing countries that are blessed with rich natural resources (hydrocarbons in particular), the struggle for power, which culminates during the election period, is essentially a fight for control over these resources. This struggle begins with the presidential elections, then the parliamentary elections – but does not extend to the municipal elections, which is quite interesting in itself. For these developing countries, their status as 'oil-extraction' countries is a basic obstacle on their path to democratic development. They are dependent on the benevolence of the West (especially the USA), because Western countries have taken it upon themselves to serve as the 'beacon' of democracy – whose rays, unfortunately, fail to reach all the countries around the globe.

Post-Soviet Examples
Of the post-Soviet countries, the 'oil-extraction' countries of Azerbaijan, Kazakhstan, Turkmenistan and Russia have, through their own experiences, proven the applicability of this trend, previously attributed only to 'third world' countries. In all post-Soviet countries with hydrocarbons we see the same picture: economic reforms are slowing down. These reforms are inhibited by the huge sums of oil-generated money, which create a false sense of security within the government. Objectively, the slower pace of economic reforms means that the oligarchic or bureaucratic capital is being strengthened. An extreme case can be seen in Turkmenistan, where all political processes have been completely frozen. Azerbaijan is a special case: the development of the oligarchic and bureaucratic capital deformed the economy and perverted society as it grew, all the while paving the way for its own self-destruction.

The political elite within these oil-extraction countries is preoccupied not with their need not to achieve political power as such – but to achieve absolute power. Their power is then sufficient enough to establish the institutions of totalitarianism (or, given the predominant democratic rhetoric in the modern world, to establish the institutions of authoritarianism). Quite naturally, such a mentality gives the ruling elite an opportunity to become associated with the very state itself, so any criticism against the authorities is automatically interpreted as an anti-state activity. Given such distorted logic, all institutions – particularly law-enforcement agencies like the police, security forces and the army – are constructed from the perspective of protecting the authorities, rather than protecting the state; and from the point of view of protecting and strengthening the regime, rather than protecting and strengthening national security. National security and, in part, internal stability, are supported at the expense of the same natural resources, with one or more influential outside actors being invited to manage these resources.

Oil and/or Democracy
The main topic of discussion amongst Azerbaijani intellectuals is 'oil and/or democracy'. This issue remains less than an attraction for both the ruling elite and the influential foreign oil companies (who came to Azerbaijan for completely different reasons than democracy). The low attractiveness of democracy means that it is often seen as an annoyance, if not a palpable headache. After all, on what level, aside from the rhetorical, can one debate and conceptualise democracy as long as the authorities are preoccupied with constantly converting the country's political resources into economic ones, and vice versa, to enable them to be both political and economic elite? Is such a profitable combination of responsibilities really possible in a democracy? How to funnel the political resources and economic flows into the sphere of power, while maintaining a dogmatic commitment to the letter of the law of democracy? What to do about the democracy 'showcase' – the presidential and parliamentary elections – knowing that the falsification of the election results, having turned into a complicated technology, requires huge financial resources, even if this might be acceptable in a country with the existing capital concentration and corruption levels?

On the other hand, 'democracy' does not mean that oil companies should permit the establishment of trade unions and their enterprises, or that these companies should acknowledge the right of local employees to strike, or to get salaries equal to those of foreign specialists. It is far easier, and cheaper, to strike a deal with the authorities. Of course, neither of the parties is interested in making the conditions of this negotiated deal known to the world democratic community, which might be shocked by the arrogance of such neo-imperialism. Those democratic countries in the West that turn a blind eye to the 'petty misdemeanours' of their oil companies (in the developing countries) have, on several occasions, become hostages to their ever-growing appetites for 'bread baked from the yeast of technology' – the desire to convert economic and political resources. Taking these scenarios out of the equation in the future, an opening for globalisation accompanied by depletion of natural resources would be possible only in the case of extreme political short-sightedness.

Capital and Politics: A Uniquely Azerbaijani Situation

As mentioned, and no matter how paradoxical it may seem, the role of capital in the political processes in Azerbaijan has not been well studied yet. Everyone knows or suspects that it plays a major role, yet it is obvious that this capital is principally acting backstage, behind the scenes. Many processes are literally replicated from one CIS country to another, but with essential differences: in the pace of institutional reforms, in the barriers to business and in the gradual reduction of the level of corruption.

The Need for a Future Direction

An obsession with the differences in the levels of development of various countries is playing a significant role in the background of the Azerbaijani situation (the situation whereby, in the next 8–10 years, Azerbaijan will rapidly grow richer). Oil revenues will then start to fall just as quickly, and, if the country has not sufficiently established an efficient export capacity by that point, one may not exclude the possibility of future, chronic economic crises. The country has little time: in the course of this decade it must manage to mobilise all its resources, if it is to mitigate future challenges and threats.

Statesmen think about the future generation, whereas politicians think about the next elections. Almost everyone understands that the country should be starting to begin its reforms today, so as not to overburden generations to come. However, the past elections, and the situation surrounding them, have shown that Azerbaijan has enough politicians – but few statesmen.

3. The Economy and the Parliamentary Elections: Connections

As explained above, this article does not analyse the purely political implications of the November parliamentary elections: it focuses only on the aspects directly related to economy. Let us simply take note of one central political and economic outcome of the last elections: yet again, the aim of creating a competitive political environment has failed, thereby jeopardising the opportunity for expanding the environment, in order for economic competition to take place in the post-election period.

Capital and the Current Elections

A New Level of Impact
On the surface, there were great similarities between the previous and current Azerbaijani elections: election fraud, an uneven playing field for the candidates during the election campaign, strict control over electronic mass media and frequent prohibitions on freedom of assembly and association. All the same, the most recent Azerbaijani parliamentary election proved unique in one sense: for the first time, capital became the most influential element of the electoral fight, and in a highly visible way. Elections are always synonymous with spending, but this time the pressure of the money was so great that some economists started to argue that the dumping of hundreds of thousands of 'shadow' dollars onto the market, in pursuit of votes, could lead to a drastic rise in prices (as quoted in the newspaper *Echo*, 3 November 2005). On the other hand, doubts have also been voiced about the ability of such short-term investments to provoke a collapse of the economy. This is an especially relevant point given that the level of inflation was not even influenced by the arrest of one of the top officials in the Azerbaijani economy.

A New Barrier to the Election Race
The paradox of the last elections, which were organised exclusively under the majority system, boiled down to the fact that, for the first time, barriers placed in the path of someone wishing to enter the electoral race proved easy to overcome. Also people with quite modest capital managed to enter the race.

Having sincerely believed in the relative fairness of the elections, such people tried to compensate for their lack of sufficient funds (for campaign advertising) through direct contact with the voters. However, the results showed that these were romanticised delusions on the part of such candidates: they found themselves in competition with a well-established state machinery, as well as with the directors of meat-processing plants, bankers, customs officials and other rich people, who had also decided to make a try in the electoral fight.

Parliamentary Composition

A Preliminary Evaluation

By preliminary evaluation (preliminary because of the additional elections of May 2006, where 10 more MPs are to be elected) the composition of the new parliament was formed by three categories of contenders:

The first group used the unlimited resources of the authorities (right down to making direct falsifications) due to their political proximity to the authorities, or to the clan.

The second group bet on capital (their own or provided), literally buying their parliamentary seats. There had already been a prior attempt to implement this kind of business project: in the 1995 elections, entrepreneurs (various rich people who, in most cases, had made their fortunes in Russia) had tried to make it into the parliament. However, they had failed, because President Heidar Aliev realised that such a parliament might not be that easy to control. Furthermore, rumours linked this scenario to Russia, and indicated that Russia wanted to have its own 'influence agents' in the parliament. Such a complicated situation was very dangerous for the authorities, which were still unstable, so the President did everything possible to block the emergence of MPs with capital in the future parliament, be it 'Azerbaijani Diaspora', or homemade 'new Azerbaijanis'.

The third, rather numerous, category in this election fight leaned on both of the previous resources. For example, oligarchs of the ruling elite put a certain number of their appointees into parliament, having supported candidates from the ruling party in return.

Other Notable Candidates

At the same time, a certain number of MPs made it to parliament without having the support of the authorities. This was because it was simply convenient for the authorities: selection was based on the loyalty of these individuals, and, in special cases, by the need to demonstrate a 'democratic' entourage. Elements of this kind of entourage are also seen in the 'professional' composition of the new parliament: formally, it has 23 lawyers and 17 economists – not a small figure for a parliament consisting of only 125 MPs. However, it seems that brilliant lawyers and smart economists were left out.

'Economic' Election Developments

Yet another 'economic' novelty of the recent elections was the change in the behaviour of major capital. The death of Heidar Aliev made it possible for many representatives of the ruling clan to breathe freely, giving them a chance to play an independent game. Indeed, some of them have, for quite some time and with a measure of success, used these new opportunities to improve their political and economic resources. The drastic exacerbation of the pre-election situation has shown just how seriously this new threat (deriving from their own 'tributaries') was taken by the authorities. The game might have become even crueller, but President Ilham Aliev managed to intervene in a timely manner. The arrests of the Minister of Economic Development and the Minister of Health, as well as of the former Minister of Finance, on charges of conspiring to overthrow the current authorities, delivered sizeable dividends to the president. The majority of these people (and those arrested later) fell victim to the political turbulence in the country, caused by the pre-election situation.

4. Arrests of Influential Actors: Background

Initial Reactions

A 'Conspiracy' Theory
Initially, the arrests had the effect of an exploding bomb. They had a significant impact on the pre-election situation, and they even caused a degree of confusion. An unexpected approach was found within the mood of the voters, and a certain strategic plan began to develop with regard to radical changes in the political situation in Azerbaijan). Perhaps this plan was drafted with the help of Russia: the influence of this country on the authorities of Azerbaijan grew after the events in October, whereas the influence of the USA declined.

The authorities skilfully bundled all their potential and real opponents into one conspiracy scenario, having declared the day of the arrival of the former Speaker of the parliament, Rasul Guliev, as the beginning of a coup d'état, financed and prepared by the arrested ministers. But: could the Minister of Economic Development, Farhad Aliev, really have been a member of a conspiracy? Was there any reason for him to undertake this dangerous role? Just like the arrested executive manager of the presidential administration (Akif Muradverdiev), the Minister of Health (Ali Insanov) did not conceal his opposition to the president, and he – at least theoretically – could be considered to be a member of a conspiracy on the basis of one of the clan's principles.

In fact, by that time, rumours had been flying around for over a year which suggested that the President had decided to reject the services of the second 'clan pillar' of the authorities (people Armenia), and these rumours were confirmed by several steps which were then taken. By contrast, Farhad Aliev seemed to behave within the framework of the general line of the Azerbaijani bureaucrat-oligarchs: almost all of them, explicitly or implicitly, tried to get their appointees into the parliament. This was no secret, and, until recently, the authorities did not see any crime in it (apart from one occasion when the President did advise the officials to steer clear of politics). The euphoric unity of the authorities during the period of presidential elections had passed; Ilham Aliev probably realised that new centres of power were emerging in the country, and that it would be possible to manage these new centres using his fa-

ther's old methods. It is the specificity of the symbiosis of politics and economy of Azerbaijan that led to a simple conclusion: when you have a lot of free
money, you do not have to 'put all your eggs into one basket'. Furthermore,
this conclusion involved the realisation that any capital is unprotected until it
has created a system with the political guarantees necessary to protect itself.
The mistake of the former minister was that, through his political games, he
raised his profile too much (but, alas, not enough for the West), and suddenly
became seen as a reformer, who, though not good for a rotation, was at least
good enough to the frighten president. This was considered to be transgress-
ing the permissible limits of ambition, and thus required public persecution
and punishment (which he did indeed receive). This managed to cut, in one
blow, all the Gordian knots that existed in the standoff between the authorities
and the opposition, and with its own intra-clan 'dissidents'.

'Political Corruption'

Interestingly, the authorities have not yet selected the final explanation for
their own 'autumn cleansing'. Once again, propaganda has been portraying
these events as if a major anti-state conspiracy had been uncovered and that
the country was embarking on a large-scale fight against corruption. The former theory requires solid proof, whereas the latter is the continuation of the
campaign (which naturally gains momentum among out-of-favour members of
the royal court). Perhaps this is why the situation remains unclear and the further development of these events seems in jeopardy. Government propaganda specialists have even created the term 'political corruption', although
nobody can really explain just what it is supposed to mean.

Political In-Fighting

The recent heavy fighting between the heads of the MED and the State Customs Committee had to end up with one of them losing. Farhad Aliev lost,
having publicly stated, not long before the arrest, that threats had been made
against his life. He even approached the Ministry of the Interior on these
grounds. The sacking of the minister had been discussed for quite a long
time, but his arrest came as a surprise to everyone.

Arrests and other Relevant Events

Regardless of whatever may or may not have occurred, the murder of the prominent Azerbaijani journalist Elmar Guseynov, as well as the discovery of a gang belonging to police officer Gadzhi Mamedov (involved in high-profile murders and racketeering), and the consequent arrests of several highly-placed officials of the Ministry of Interior, stand out as events which indicated yet another major political crisis. The effects were eased by the consequent election collisions, but the political and economic echoes will linger for quite a while.

The Arrest of Farhad Aliev

The arrest of Farhad Aliev, who held many of the keys to the Azerbaijani economy, could not help but have significant consequences. This is so, even though Heidar Babayev was appointed to his position on the same day, and Babayev, as the head of the Central Bank, is well-versed in economic issues.

Farhad Aliev and Azpetrol

The private Azpetrol holding, formerly headed by the brother of the Ministry of the Economy (he was also arrested), is a basic element of the Azerbaijani economic system. It was officially founded in 1999 on the basis of several existing companies, and almost certainly enjoyed the support of Farhad Aliev, even though Rafik Aliev was a capable and energetic businessman. It has huge assets at its disposal – according to some assessments, amounting to as much as USD 250 million, plus the new assets of the holding in Moldova. The total assets of the Farhad Aliev clan, from the under-represented ruling power in the southern region (the Jalilabad), exceed the stated figure several times over (perhaps more than 1 billion USD). Obviously, to destroy such an industrial and financial empire would be extremely irrational. It is no less obvious that such major assets would become the subject of severe redistribution. It is not by accident that, in the Russian press, Azpetrol has been called the Azerbaijani YUKOS (although comparing M. Khodorkovsky and F. Aliyev would not be proper, as they are personalities of different scales). But the legal dilemma is not that simple either. So far, it is not clear how one

could take these assets away, since the company has been working trans-
parently, with annual audits and its practice of providing creditors with the lists
of shareholders of the company. In recent years, moreover, it has been an
active partner of EBRD, and the top manager of this holding was the former
EBRD representative in the country, Thomas Moser. It appears that, for this
reason, the company is still alive, and has been trying to support its activities
by making counter-statements to the information given by the authorities.
Farhad Aliev himself refuses to answer the questions of the investigators, and
has not pleaded guilty. Theoretically, nationalisation of the company is possible, as would be transferring its management over to the state, but this could
cause negative reactions on the part of foreign investors. However, the first
step has already been taken: the shares of the company have been transferred to Ibragim Mamedov, who used to own only 5% in one of the companies of this holding. This was because the Arbitration Court viewed the complicated structure of re-documenting property as a violation of the rights of
one of the owners, and as elements of an irregular deal.

Farhad Aliev and Other Companies
Other events have followed. For example, the country may lose Barmek, a
company that, four years ago, won a tender for the management of the electricity distribution networks of the capital, as well as Sumgait and the districts
of Azerbaijan to the north of Baku. The company, headed by Gusein Abdulov
(a Turk), not only improved the supply of electricity, it also began actively introducing a European management system, to make it transparent within society and in its contractual relations with the government. On the other hand,
the work of a distribution company indirectly exposed weaknesses in electricity generation, which has remained in the hands of the government. This
could not help but cause frustration in the ministerial offices: some of their
representatives even demanded that this company leave the country. And
here we should note that Farhad Aliev was the patron of this company.

Currently a struggle is taking place against all the companies or enterprises
that are related, to any degree, to the former minister. Active inspections of
Azeralumini are underway. Compared to the troubles of AzPetrol, the legal
situation here is simpler: the metallurgical complex has formally been given
up in favour of management, and the state has the ability to cancel the rele-

vant contract. Judging by the sudden visit of the UK-based billionaire industrialist Lakshmi Narayan Mittal to Azerbaijan, who has just bought the Ukrainian industrial giant 'Krivorozhstal' for 4.2 billion USD, he probably intends to work in the Azerbaijani non-ferrous metals industry. The deal with such a major businessman would, of course, partially reduce the negative effects of the persecution of the disfavoured team.

The Redistribution of Property
However, a negative point about redistribution of property is that it can be hard to know where to stop. Work is now underway with some quite successful privatised enterprises: Baku electric stamping plant (Bakelectrostamp) and Baku steel-smelting plant (Bakipoladtekme). Their owner, Zulfugarly, and his brothers, have been arrested. At the same time, an investigation is underway concerning the cable and isolate plant in Mingechaur, the NCT plant, which produces plastic pipes. Once again, this involves successful enterprises that have started to export their products.

One could argue that the series of PR campaigns pursued by the former minister will cease. These campaigns have involved the distribution of money under the auspices of NFPP, city fairs under the motto 'Buy homemade goods', and finally, the lack of a fight against monopolies. From the point of view of a monopoly, Farhad Aliyev was no angel, but he did imitate anti-monopoly activities and thus drew interest towards this topic.

A Final Note
It is unlikely that the changes now underway in the structure of the authorities will pass painlessly. Even the destruction of a bad system may cause problems. Nevertheless, we can trace a natural conformity behind all these events. The vertical line of power in Azerbaijan is growing stronger, and everything that might possibly hinder this – also within the ruling clan – will be ruthlessly suppressed. In this consolidation there is no room for 'potential outsiders'.

5. The new Parliament: Current State of Affairs

Initial Optimism

Optimists pinned great hopes on the recent parliamentary elections. They counted on the renewed parliament not only to be able have a greater impact on the activities of the government (such as control of the government, and the budget), but also to bring better order to legislative activities in the sphere of the economy. For example, it was hoped that the new parliament would establish clearer control over those legislative acts that ensure implementation of relevant laws, as it is in this area that legislation has a very difficult time. And yet, just a year before the elections, these expectations proved illusory. The previous parliament calmly passed the law on banks, without daring to discuss – even theoretically – the subordination of the national bank to the parliament. Similarly, important laws were discarded, among them 'On investment activities', 'On oil and gas', an Anti-monopoly code, and 'On education'. All talk about the possible development of the law 'On the oil fund' ceased. Even the Western financial structures that had been insistent on the latter question stopped raising this issue, limiting themselves to the EITI ('extracting industry transparency initiative'), which had been proposed a few years ago by British prime minister Tony Blair. It became obvious that the ruling elite did not intend, under any circumstances, to part with its control over the financial flows in the country. The optimists have been disgraced, and it is unlikely that the new parliament will be any better than the previous one. Furthermore, a 'semi-oligarch' has been put in the seat of the Speaker, having bought the victory in his constituency.

Comparative Perspective

Kazakhstan
The results of Azerbaijan's elections are also interesting from a comparative point of view. The same optimists could have noticed that, despite its authoritarian regime, Kazakhstan has managed to make significant economic progress. Especially important is the fact that this progress was achieved not

only thanks to the high GDP indicators and industrial capacity growth rates (which is quite natural, given the oil prices), but also thanks to the constant interest of the President towards institutional reforms in the economy, or at least to the point where they do not threaten the authoritarian regime itself. Since it is unknown where this limit is, the regime is nevertheless rocked by the new realities.[1] Moreover, the scale of the changes and the intelligence of the Kazakh President seem to have worked. Willingly or unwillingly, he has created an excellent economic basis for the future democracy. Kazakhstan has implemented a great number of reformist steps that Azerbaijan has not yet made, or is just beginning to make. This country created the best banking system in the CIS. The implementation of an accumulative pension insurance scheme started back in 1997, and the practice of mortgaging housing is working. Kazakhstan has long entered into international financial markets, and is successfully developing its own financial market as well.

General Note on Comparisons
It is traditional that, when considering someone else's experience, the authorities, and a significant portion of our society, tend to concentrate on the negative points, ignoring the positive elements. In the new Georgian democracy, one notes the reduced living standards of the population, but ignores the fact that, in 2005, the Georgian budget was comparable to that of Azerbaijan, and that this was achieved not only with the help of external aid, but also through the implementation of a strict budget policy and by the suppression of corruption. It seems that we do not wish to notice the vital factors. Just as in Ukraine, the Georgian supreme power has definitely become 'changeable', and for the indefinite future, nobody will be able to usurp it.

Russia
With this in mind, we should note that this article is only attempting to borrow the worst political experiences of Russian 'guided democracy' (i.e. the vertical management of the country, the elimination of the opposition, and the control over electronic mass media). No attention is paid to the important changes

---

1   See D. Furman, 'Post-Soviet regime in Kazakhstan', compendium *Kazakhstan and Russia*, 2004, Moscow.

taking place in Russian education, science and healthcare. The target setting in the Russian economy does limit itself to poverty reduction. It also implies that a comprehensive Russian development strategy has been created up until 2025 (which additionally implies that we are searching for Russia's place both in the world and in the explosive technological advances). The appearance of such an economic doctrines shows the viability of the Russian elite (of both the pro-authorities and the anti-authorities), and also indicates the unspoken but constructive dialogue between these elite.[2] Nothing of this kind exists, or is anticipated, in Azerbaijan – and this is the fault of the authorities.

Of course, in Russia, this is accompanied by a crude redistribution of property, in favour of the bureaucracy. But this country has definitely gone down the road from oligarchic to bureaucratic capitalism. In Azerbaijan, there has been no 'oligarchic' capital by definition: as we have seen, economic power is inseparable from political power, and this results in the presence of oligarchic-bureaucratic capitalism. Azerbaijan has never had 'Russian-style' relations between the business and the authorities. Capital was formed by the bureaucracy, who were fully subordinate to the top person in the country; for that reason, one could never imagine, even hypothetically, a dialogue between the authorities and business. Interestingly, in the 1999 World Bank evaluation, under the 'power capture' index, Azerbaijan ranked number 1, whereas Armenia ranked last.[3] The situation has not changed significantly since that time, since business has merged even more closely with the authorities.

Nevertheless, the ideas of democracy come across as insuperable. In Russia itself, many observers note that the Putin model of reforms will sooner or later face obstacles of a fundamental nature, as the development of the country is impossible without the establishment of a self-regulating and fairly open system. The fairly rationally current working system, trying to reach a balance between the bankrupting of YUKOS by the liberalisation of Gazprom shares, and the suppression of freedom by the establishment of the public chamber, is already in trouble.[4]

---

2   *Expert* magazine, 45, 2005, p. 25.
3   World Bank Policy Research Working Paper, April 2000, p. 24.
4   E. Yasin. Whether democracy will find its place in Russia, 2005, Moscow.

The Path of Azerbaijan

To return to Azerbaijan: its thorny path to democracy is imposed by the gradual economic advancements that arguably automatically lead to Western standards of political life. Let us take a look at whether this path is possible in principle, given that other paths are not considered an option by the authorities and the West – in this case, the USA.

6. The Azerbaijani Economy: Finally on the Path to Democracy

'Economy First, then Democracy'

The President of the country frequently refers to a formula (by his father) that has become quite common in the post-Soviet environment: first, we need to improve the economy of the country, and only then can we think about democracy. In 2004, the President repeated this fairly simple thesis in Strasbourg, during a speech in front of the representatives of the European Parliament. In fact, the development of the economy in this area was not really the fruits of the efforts of the entire society, but rather 'manna from heaven' that should fall upon Azerbaijan. And this is what is happening, to a certain degree.

Positive Indications

The main macro-economic indicators of the country seem to point to an excellent situation. Total GDP growth in 2005 will, it seems, have achieved about 26% growth. Furthermore, relative industrial output growth is expected to reach more than 33%.[5] The income of the population is outpacing inflation. In terms of investment (the investment growth rate over the 11 months of 2005 was only 11.9%, three times lower than last year), the economy is shifting into the mode of sustainable revenues from the oil sector and there has been growth in domestic investments. Wonderful new perspectives seem to be opening up for the country.

The Need for Balance

The implementation of projects like the Baku–Tbilisi–Ceyhan or the Baku–Tbilisi–Erzurum gas pipeline clearly mark a new milestone in the development of both the Southern Caucasus and the entire Caspian region. The decade-long epic, full of internal drama, is now over. Over these years, Azerbaijan

---

5   As presented by the State Statistics Committee of Azerbaijan, *Macroeconomic indicators for January–November 2005.*

quite often gave in to the FOC. Some of this was inevitable, whilst some could have been avoided, had there been enough political will. But this is all in the past, and a new starting point for the economic history of Azerbaijan will now be witnessed. One reason for this might be that the country's approximate oil and gas reserves have been calculated (excluding unforeseen situations), and that the nature of relations in this sphere has started to change. On the one hand, in the future, Azerbaijan will face the need for cautious and efficient use of the flow of oil dollars which will hit the country very soon, and all attention is now concentrated on the state oil fund. On the other hand, the revision and the evaluation of new oil and gas opportunities for the country are now underway, in particular, transit of Central Asian oil, and in the future, possibly also Russian oil.

The economic revival underway in the regions is obvious, and there have been attempts to begin implementation of a series of projects of nationwide importance. The official registration of entrepreneurs has been simplified. All these things are happening on the wave of income growth and the demands of the people. The government is raising salaries and student scholarships, but in selected narrow social groups it fears pushing up the inflation. In the last months of 2005, it was announced that the salaries of fairly large groups of public servants would be raised (by 30% for doctors). Finally, people started talking about an exchange rate adjustment for the private deposits, which is to start in 2006.

Examining the Growth Rate

However, it is not uncomplicated to believe this impressive horizon for the upcoming future. First of all, one cannot help but be confused about the abnormal nature of this growth. The growth of the budget in 2006 by almost 70% (or GDP by 30.2%) is testimony to some extraordinary processes in the economy (it is notable GDP growth rates of the coming year may rise as much as 40% if oil prices remain at a level of USD 50 per barrel). Here we may note some of the assessments made by an expert group from the Azerbaijani NGO PFMC. This assessment studies the impact of oil on the economy of the country, and is indicated below (referring to the results for 2005).

- The shares of oil and oil products in the country's exports consisted of up to 84% of the total amount.
- The share of the total investments of oil sector I consisted of up to 63.77%, and when including foreign investments, up to 86.7%.
- The shares of oil sector in the GDP rose up to 42.9%.
- The shares of oil incomes in the state budget are evaluated at a level of approximately 40–45%. It is expected that, in 2006, this figure will grow to 60%.
- Over the last 9 months of 2005, the official exchange rate of the manat against the US dollar grew stronger by 310 manats, or 6.3%, and rose to 4,593 manats.

Secondly, rapid growth is always a challenge that requires an adequate response, or else it will only deepen the social divides in society. In the absence of strong state institutions, such growth always makes the rich even richer, and the poor even poorer. Add to this the macroeconomic balance, and the situation becomes precarious indeed.

Main Macro-Economic Indicators and Azerbaijan

However, thus far, the Azerbaijani economy may also come across as very 'correct' in terms of the main globally-accepted macroeconomic indicators. Let us name these standard parameters (in italics) and evaluate the corresponding levels in Azerbaijan.

The level of the national budget deficit should not exceed 3–5% of the GDP. Over the last 8 years, it has never crossed this limit. Furthermore, in several of those years it went down to zero and even transformed itself into budget profits.

Public debt should not exceed 60% of the GDP. In Azerbaijan, it has never crossed the limit of 17%. Based on the results of this year, public debt will not exceed 15.6%. Even now, when the country has started to accumulate debt, it is unlikely that the level will cross the 25%/ GDP threshold.

The total volume of the gold reserves should be sufficient to cover the import expenditure for at least three months. Together with the oil fund, the volume of the gold reserves covers this threshold several times over (USD 2.3

billion). This even forces the Central Bank to restrain the growth in currency reserves, due to the significant growth of the price of national currency in the country.

The critical level of unemployment should not exceed 10–15% of the total able-bodied population. Official statistics do not reveal the unemployment level in the country, as they record only the number of people applying to the employment services. However, we may assume that the programme declared by the government, for the creation of 600,000 jobs (over a period of two to three years), has, to a certain degree, taken into account the real unemployment level in the country. But with no less than 1 million labour migrants outside the country (and assuming that approximately 4 million people comprise the economically active population of the country), the unemployment level is high, although not critical.

The ratio of the current payments to the servicing of the foreign debt should not exceed 20% of annual export revenues Annual payment for servicing the foreign debt varies between 1–1.5% of budget revenues, and is even less for exports.

The growth of the bulk of the cash should correspond to the growth of production. In recent years, the bulk of the cash has been growing quite rapidly (on average at a rate of 20–25% per annum). However, the one-sided, oil-based development, and the 'dollarisation' of the economy, make it difficult to assess real cash needs. It is known, however, that the rate of cash turnover (of the manat in Azerbaijan) has always been in the range of 12–17%.

To secure the investment process, the level of savings in GDP should be equal to or exceed 10%. This level has always been above 10%; in some years, since the investment component of GDP has been as much as 50% of GDP.

The share of foreign goods in individual sectors of the national market shall not exceed 10–20% etc. This indicator is poorly analysed, but many new industries have emerged in the consumer sector, so one should assume that the country is below this minimal norm.

Within the framework of these indicators, the Azerbaijani economy may come across as having good perspectives and being quite protected. However, the process of evaluating the state of the economy operates with many other parameters. For example, the banking system is small (just over 15% of

GDP), and the turnover of securities is 4.4% of GDP (largely at the expense of short-term state securities). Even after the recent rapid budget growth, the ratio of budget revenues to GDP will rise to roughly 25%. Furthermore, many social indicators of the economy are quite low. We must conclude that rumours of the wonderful health of the Azerbaijani economy are somewhat exaggerated.

7. The Economy: Regulated by whom, and how?

The Influence of the President

It appears that the answer to the question of who regulates the Azerbaijani economy, and how, may boil down to the unlimited authority of the president, who easily exceeds the boundaries of the constitutional framework when he considers it necessary. And from this perspective it is not difficult to explain the excessive authority of the president's administration, which co-ordinates all spheres of life in the country. However, in practice, the economy requires a constant professional approach other than the bureaucratic one.

Agency Relations

The system of relations between the agencies responsible for the economy of Azerbaijan is not a simple one. It is a paradox, but the chairman of the Cabinet of Ministers is a purely nominal figure who governs but does not rule. The 'economic' deputy ministers perform the duties of assignees in various sectors of the economy, although they all have a different weight in decision-making process (the problems and crisis situations of agriculture and the food market were within the realm of the first deputy prime minister, Abas Abasov, whereas construction, foreign credit lines, and, until recently, emergencies, were controlled by the deputy prime minister, Abid Sharifov). Other deputy prime ministers are either involved in humanitarian issues, or are merely nominal figures – like deputy prime minister Eyub Yagubov, formally responsible for industry and energy. Importantly, Azerbaijan has no deputy prime minister responsible for the financial sector, although would certainly be appropriate in the new conditions.

The Prime Minister and Others

The power of the prime minister is limited by the president, as well as his administration (at the top of the scale), and by various fairly influential and wealthy independent figures of the economic establishment (at the bottom of the scale). The most influential personalities in the management of the Azerbaijani economy are the Minister of Economic Development, Heidar Babayev, and the head of the Azerbaijani customs, Kyamaletdin Heidarov (who was recently appointed Minister of Emergencies and vacated his previous position in favour of his deputy). The exclusiveness of these people is explained not only by their significant capital, but also by their proximity to the president. All the other economic agencies of the country are, to a greater or lesser degree, part of the range of the above-mentioned entities. The National Bank might have been another influential economic decision-making centre, but its direct subordination to the nation's President significantly lowers its capabilities. On the other hand, the deteriorating macro-economic situation in the country will serve to brings the National Bank to greater prominence.

The 2006 Budget: Current Forecasts

And what of the budget of the country for 2006? Its growth is quite impressive, although, in comparison to the other CIS countries, budget revenues are low indeed: just over 3 billion new manats (1 'new' manat is equal to 5000 'old' mantas, at the exchange rate of 4500 old manat to one dollar used in the budget).[6] The budget deficit is not to exceed 1.3% of GDP.

A peculiar feature of the 2006 budget is that investment expenditures are set to grow by 3.8 times. USD 450–600 million will be spent on improving the delivery of energy alone, and about USD 600 million will go to military expenditures. Declared budget priorities are as follows: development of the non-oil sector, tourism, entrepreneurial support and support for national industries, poverty reduction, regional development, as well as the development of the banking and the financial sectors. The latter, as a rule, did away without budget support, usually relying solely on the placement of budget organisation resources within the banking system. However, the establishment of the home mortgage fund made the country face up to the need to support the charter capital of the new structure, which will rise to about 130 billion 'old' manat. Budget funds have also been allocated for the establishment of the charter capital of the State Investment Fund.

---

6   As quoted from 'The law on the budget of the AR for 2006', *Halg gazeti*.

The 2006 Budget: Grounds for Concern

Investment Wastage

Many economists are concerned about the increased investment component of the budget, which, under regular conditions, should actually be a source of optimism. There are solid grounds for this concern. In fact, neither the treasury nor the chamber of accounts (which is not even admitted over the threshold of many major ministries), work to their full capacity in Azerbaijan.[7] In these circumstances, the probability of a situation whereby investment is corruptly wasted is very high indeed.

Transparency

There are other worrying points about the 2006 budget that have to do with its transparency. In accordance with the law on the budget system, at the time of drafting the budget it is mandatory that the revenues and expenditures be disclosed. The 2006 budget elaborates on all budget expenditure items in a fair amount of detail, but budget revenue structures remain a closed subject – not so surprisingly, since it is within the expenditure part that the inflation threats are hidden. The structure of expenditures seems to include an entire set of anti-inflation measures. As far as the revenue part is concerned, it becomes obvious that the authorities are attempting to conceal the fact that a portion of the 2006 budget revenues will be created at the expense of oil revenues. On several occasions, the Minister of Finance stated that budget growth would rise to 40%, even when excluding transfers from the oil fund. However, in such a case, it becomes unclear why one had to resort to these emergency and dangerous (from a macroeconomic point of view) infusions. According to some scrupulous calculations, the growth of the 2006 budget will rise to up to 85%, depending on oil (i.e. on high oil prices and a transfer from the SOFAR). Of course, the rapid growth of the budget was dictated by the pre-election situation, which demanded victorious deeds, and this is why, in the next few years, these growth rates will most likely return to a more realistic level. It appears that this is a minor act of slyness on the part of govern-

---

7   *Turan Economic Monthly Review*, September 2005.

ment, who do not want to reveal just how dependent the economy is on the oil factor. However, here we should recall the recent statement of the head of the Chamber of Accounts, who believes that the basic 'budgeting feed' of corruption stems from this badly formulated revenue part of the budget. This is related both to the shadow sector of the economy, and also to the complicated budget relations within the oil and energy sector of the country. In other words, the debt within the energy sector completely overshadows the activities of these major enterprises and paves the road towards financial abuse. The exaggerated costs of several major state companies and the growth of the prime costs of produced goods (hardly assessed by anyone) result in a reduction in budget revenues. Here we could recall the statistics of the high social taxes, which indicated that 1.4 million people were covered by this tax, whereas the economically active population of the country is roughly 4 million. Unaccounted jobs are the shortfalls of the budget.

Unrealistic Forecasting

Economists are doubtful about the predicted oil price, as calculated in the budget. If retail prices for crude oil exceed the USD 40/barrel in 2006, as included in the budget, then the additional export revenue will be distributed between SOCAR and SOFAR on a 50/50 basis. If the retail prices for crude oil exceed USD 50, than the State Oil Fund will receive 75% of the difference, and state oil company will receive 25%.

Growing oil revenues predetermine the fact that the development of the banking sector a top item on the agenda. It is developing rapidly, and could even be a source of pride for the government, were it not for the shocking parallels with the banking systems of other countries. We shall not touch on Kazakhstan, whose banking system has long been acknowledged as the best in the CIS. At one meeting in 2005, the IMF representative in Baku, Bezil Zavoiko, reminded us that the capitalisation of the largest bank in Estonia (with a population 4 or 5 times less than in Azerbaijan) is three times higher than the capitalisation of the Azerbaijani monster, i.e. the international bank.[8] It is obvious that this cannot be not related to the institutional development of the entire Estonian economy, including the banking sector. For this reason,

---

8   *Turan Economic Monthly Review*, September 2005.

there is nothing surprising about the fact that the volume of the banking market, as against GDP, is only 16%, although very recently it had been below 10%.

Lack of Alternative Sources for Borrowing

Azerbaijan also lacks alternative sources for borrowing. This means that the price of money in the country is not elastic, and that the banking sector plays the role of a single legislator (in terms of the price of money in the country), and that this deprives the financial system of necessary elasticity. Other sources of financial resources (such as the stock market, insurance market, pension funds) are formed very slowly. Half of the turnover of the stock exchange was made up of transactions with state securities, whilst the rest was formed by corporate shares and bank bonds, and just as small a fraction were shares of enterprises. The entire turnover of the stock market in 2005 rose to roughly 4.4% of GDP. The insurance market in the country is even smaller (0.8% of the GDP). Of course, the insurance market is growing, but two thirds of these resources will be channelled to foreign insurance companies for re-insurance. As to the pension fund, it may become a financial pillar for the economy only after the completion of the pension reform, set to start in 2006.

8. New Challenges – Old Answers

Banking

Throughout 2005, the National Bank of Azerbaijan (NBA) acted as a centre forward in fighting inflation, by raising the price of the national currency. It undertook this role eagerly, deviating from the more detailed and complicated tasks that are within its competence (for example, reforms of the financial system, furnishing it with the ability to transform savings into investments). Strengthening the national currency is the easiest way to fight inflation, but it exacerbates the lack of competitiveness of Azerbaijani goods on foreign markets. For this reason, the government resorted to a wide range of anti-inflation measures, and the President was even forced to issue a special decree on this matter. The NBA also tried to address some of its problems. In particular, the growing value of the manat may reduce the dollar turnover in the country. As of early December 2005, foreign currency deposits in the banking system rose to 81.2%, [9] which is very important, given the background of the denomination of the manat as of 1 January 2006. Although denomination is usually a mere technical exercise, judging by the experience of the other countries, it may give room for inflation, although the central bank has issued reassurances that this 'technical inflation' will not exceed 1% of total inflation.

The banking sphere is always reproached for failing to perform its basic function: crediting the real sector of the economy. Bankers commonly reply that industrial production in the country is underdeveloped and, even given enough resources, they would not be able to find sufficiently efficient projects for crediting. As far as the active work of the banks with small and medium-sized enterprises, or with the agricultural sector, it is related to the fact that external creditors can be found for these projects, and such crediting is performed at their expense. Annual customs reviews show that the share of oil and oil products has, in recent years, been at a sustainable level of between 85 and 90% all export.[10]

---

9   See the website of the national bank of Azerbaijan, at http://www.nba.az
10   Foreign trade review, 'Customs' newspaper, *Komruk*, 23 December 2005.

Development of the Non-Oil Sector

It is self-evident that the country needs to develop the non-oil section of its exports. Possible points for a breakthrough here include non-ferrous metals, oil machinery, oil chemicals, construction materials, and a whole series of agricultural sub-sectors. To the already familiar construction boom, we should add the growth of the new enterprises producing construction materials, in the capital and elsewhere in the country. The significant growth of the number of these enterprises is, quite naturally, a response to the boom in housing construction. Agricultural processing started to develop quite rapidly. Among the positive developments, we may note a significant growth in leasing transactions. The aggregate capitol of the leasing portfolio of companies active in Azerbaijan has already reached USD 25 million, whereas the total capacity of this market is evaluated at USD 250 million (although in the latter case we are talking mostly about the development of agricultural leasing). However, any move toward exporting is practically impossible without powerful protection. Furthermore, Azerbaijan already has quite powerful conglomerates, in the form of financial and industrial groups (FIG), capable of controlling both the import and export of goods – and every FIG has a connection to the name of some minister-oligarch. To a certain degree, this explains why the government has not been willing to address problems that were seemingly on the surface – from promoting the packing industry, to the normal functioning of the Export Promotion Fund. The country has no industrial policy, and it is unlikely to have one in the foreseeable future.

Economic Axioms

Many economic principles are axioms. For example, it is well known that it is better to import capital into the country rather than goods, that it is better to import new technologies and equipment than readymade goods, and that direct investments are always better than credits and loan. However, from the very beginning, the Azerbaijani economic system was formed in such a way that individual economic groups were given the opportunity to have a free rein. This is where the sad results enter: the customs are too powerful and controlled, whereas, on the other hand, the banking system is weak, has a hard time getting the right to borrow from global financial markets, and is barely capable of adapting to major inflows of capital. Furthermore, the entire structure of economic management has been distorted, and many ministries keep on acting both as of regulators of the relations in an industry, and as proprietors. A whole series of ministries and agencies function as the oligarch's 'backyard'.

This is how the situation usually works: initially, the state structures start to shape up around the minister (as they are quite easily controlled by the minister himself). Then a structure evolves whereby private holdings emerge, where capital is being transferred, as well as private construction companies or networks of stores. Here we should mention the 'offshore effect', whereby the major capital initially leaves the territory of the country, and then returns into the country in the form of an offshore foreign firm. For this reason, a real foreign investor cannot enter any segment of the market without having a contact with one of the oligarchs who controls this sector of economy. The President of the country also has direct access, but his position is frequently predetermined by the position of influential groups and agencies and private interests.

Relations between the State and Foreign Companies

A Complicated Relationship

Relations between the state and foreign companies have recently been characterised by complications. Of course, sooner or later these relationships had to acquire a working nature, with all the relevant consequences. But the presence of open pressure on various foreign companies (outside of the oil sector, of course) can already be felt. How to explain this new phenomenon in the Azerbaijani economy? This is most likely because the 'fat' that shaped and formed oligarchic economy feels cramped in its established limits, and strives to expand its field of activity. At the same time, any unlawfulness is perceived by foreign investors as a danger signal. Furthermore, the visible hassle within the authorities can scarcely act as an attraction for foreign incentives – especially since several laws that would provide both an incentive and a protection for foreign investments have not been passed after all.

Foreign Investors: The Superficial Impression
On the surface, Azerbaijan formally remains an attractive country for foreign investors. The total gold reserves (when calculated jointly with the oil fund) are at present 2.3 billion USD.[11] By mid-2005, the foreign debt of the country had already fallen by USD 86 million and is at present only USD 1,502 billion. Some capital has come into the country, but nobody dares to have major direct investments, and no one will. What serious investor will come to a country where the judiciary is underperforming, where there is no competitive environment, and where monopolies rule? Many potential investors know that they will face the resistance of the serious monopoly groups, controlled by members of the government itself.

Constant Need for New Solutions

The Anti-Monopoly Department of the Ministry of Economic Development
Furthermore, today the mere recording of new opportunities is not enough, and there is a need for a constant search for new solutions. We could mention the activities of the anti-monopoly department of the Ministry of Economic Development as an example. Some time ago, there was a separate anti-monopoly committee, directly subordinate to the President of the country. Then for some reason it was merged with the Ministry of Economic Development. Recently, this department has been monitoring the monopoly spheres, without overburdening itself by presenting proposals to reduce the level of monopolisation, even in the spheres where this would be possible. At the same time, today there are plenty of real proposals already. For example, take cement production, where a real deficit can be observed, due to the construction boom: a group consisting of an Azerbaijani, a Chinese and an Iranian company are ready to create to the new cement enterprises in the country, and a German company is ready to supply modern equipment in order to produce this cement.[12] The real anti-monopoly policy boils down to the fol-

---

11   See http://www.nba.az
12   Turan Monthly Economic Review, June 2005.

lowing: it uses the mechanisms of power (privileges, tax preferences etc.) in order to reduce the pressure and tension in a certain market segment, support new industries and enterprises as a counterbalance to the older ones, and eventually create a competitive environment. But for all this to happen, the anti-monopoly agency needs to have high status, including access to the top person in the country.

Providing Foreign Investors with the Necessary Demand
As a rule, investors are attracted to sufficiently large markets. If the country is small, it is of key importance for the investor to enjoy a high demand in the country, to compensate for the insufficient physical volume of the market. Recently, demand has grown somewhat, but the level of poverty remains very high, even though through some miracle the authorities reduced poverty down to 29% in 2004.

The Creation of New Jobs
In order for a breakthrough to occur, structural reforms, normal relations between business and the authorities, a well-conceived investment policy and the creation of new jobs are required. In the last case, there seems to have been some progress, as over the past two years, the country would appear to have created 300,000 new jobs. In one of the most recent statements made by the president, a figure of 340,000 was even mentioned.[13] However, the concept of a 'job' is so vague that we could boldly divide this figure by two, if not by four. Judging by the official data, only half of them are permanent jobs, and from the remaining half, we should subtract those with extremely low productivity, or those of people on the verge of becoming redundant. It is enough to say that a visible portion of the jobs is created in the agricultural sector, where the number of working people generally always includes the number of families in the households, who in actual fact already participate in the economic activities.

---

13   *Bakinsky rabochy*, 30 December 2005.

Lessening the Reliance on Oil

Oil creates the illusion that any problem may be addressed, since big money is coming into the country. With regard to industrial production, the constant pedalling of GDP growth becomes not only senseless, but also dangerous. No less than a third of GDP growth relates to oil, and the plan is to cover the anticipated reduction in investment expected in the next few years by using the growing IFI loans.

Many economists are asking themselves: are the rapidly growing oil prices capable of compensating for the reduction in investments? Most of them say 'no', since, from the point of view of content, these resources create excessive consumption, inflation and imports. For many reasons, the economy does not manage to spend this money quickly enough.

Global oil prices keep growing, opening new perspectives for the government. First, there is an opportunity for all the investment expenses of AMOC to be paid off in advance, and this means that, in the immediate future, the state share in the profitable oil may become quite impressive. Secondly, beginning in 2006, the state budget will be receiving a tax on AMOC profits, and this amount may rise to USD 220 million.

It may well be that the authorities are lucky – but they have as yet to prove that it is the entire society of Azerbaijan that is lucky. The economy is entering a turbulent time in its development. There will be many problems related to the growing exchange rate of the manat (even today an entrepreneur that had received a cheap manat loan will have to repay it using the manat of a higher value), the balance of payments (there will be no deficit in the trade balance, but investment incomes leaving the country will grow significantly). And the newly created jobs may disappear just as quickly as they appeared.

People still speak of the 'Holland syndrome' with caution, although all the classical signs of this illness are evident: the shift of the economy into consumption mode, the unstoppable growth of value of the national currency, and the lack of control over the government. The chances of a Holland syndrome appearing have been questioned by prominent Azerbaijani economist Ogtay Ahverdiev, who believes that this is impossible, due to a wide array of production activities represented in the country.[14] This much-debated syn-

---

14   See http://www.day.az

drome initially appears in an economy in connection to the imperatives of the exchange rate policy, so such optimism would seem somewhat naive.

The Mid-Term Perspective

From a mid-term perspective, the developmental direction of the country has become more precise – in its statements, as well as in its confident reliance on the transit capacities of the country, the development of its internal infrastructure in the broadest meaning of the word, and the SME development.

In these circumstances, is it possible to reform the economic system whilst avoiding political turbulence? This is the question of the day. It is also important to bear in mind that the price of every mistake in the economic development of Azerbaijan is becoming much higher. The difference between the new opportunities for the country and its institutional underdevelopment has already become too apparent.

The Public and Private Sectors: a Remaining Lack of Balance

The country has still failed to find a balance between the expanding private sector in the economy and the state-run part of the economy. The latter part is still great. There are levers of administrative influence at its disposal, which it can put to active use in order to reconfirm its position of monopoly – as it also does in the private sector.

The Judiciary: Problems

The judiciary is the target of the vast majority of the entrepreneurs' complaints, as it visibly hinders business development. The new head of the Supreme Court has tried to explain the system of bribery that exists in courts by a 'low level of awareness' among entrepreneurs. However, the latter group are confident that even the most justified dispute of any decision needs to be 'reconfirmed' by providing a bribe to the court. They also argue that any dispute with a state agency or enterprise, or with the major monopolists, is *a priori* doomed to failure. Additional opportunities for abuse are created by the lack of regulation as to how long it takes for a court case to be resolved. At the same time, instead of considering this factor in such cases to be an oversight of the compliance with procedural norms, the courts of higher instance consider it to be part of the essence of the case itself, which in turn leads to court cases taking a great deal of time to solve it. Some cases have been considered by various instances some 60 to 70 times. According to Alekper Mamedov, Head of the Association of Entrepreneurs of Azerbaijan, roughly 30 cases have been deemed by the constitutional court of the country to be not in compliance with the Constitution. This should mean one thing: the case should be resolved in favour of the appealing party. But this does not happen. Furthermore, total confusion exists in the execution of judicial verdicts and decisions.

Inflation

It is premature to speak of the problems of inflation in the past tense. This factor is seemingly the reverse side of economic growth, but nevertheless the government proved unprepared for it. It is in this realm that we once again become witnesses to the backwardness of the institutional mechanisms in the financial system.

Quite a few countries have tripped up on the reforms of the utilities that usually provoke inflation. In the case of Azerbaijan, we could say that this part of the reform is just beginning. The growth of tariffs for electricity, gas and water is inevitable. For the latter two, this has already started and is expected to continue. The state has been reassured that this practice not only leads to a rise in prices, but that it also increases inflation expectations. However, the state has not realised – or rather it does not want to realise – that one should prepare for such reforms in advance. In the end, in the scale of the infrastructural preparations which are necessary, the process of installing electricity, gas and water meters is insignificant. Yet there is a critical lack of them, because the moment for their installation was lost, and it has now become difficult to assess the real needs of the country and its people in relation to the sources of energy.

A Final Analysis

Over the recent years, when GDP per capita has been at USD 1,517, the government has constantly declared that the people of Azerbaijan hold the world record in investment growth rates, GDP and budget revenues (depending on which indicator looks most impressive at any given time). The Ministry of Finance reported that, in 2006, Azerbaijan will be number one in the world in terms of GDP growth rates. This, of course, reflects the country's growing (and short-term) contribution to the global economy. However, the citizens of the country are entitled to ask, 'Well, what does that mean for us?' and the answer will make hardly anyone happy: nothing, or almost nothing. Economic growth is taking place not thanks to the reforms, or to increased productivity, but due to the rising oil prices. And this makes the economy highly vulnerable, while the increased pace of this growth requires a completely different fine-tuning of the economy and other work with society.

It is for this reason that society barely shares the official optimism. For example, it seems that despite the growth in the average wage in the country (USD 127), the quality of life is not improving to any notable degree. The number of social threats and worries has grown. The opportunity for a person to make a rapid horizontal or vertical movement across the social categories of the country is visibly limited by corruption. Corruption rules, having penetrated the most sensitive pores of the social organism: education, healthcare, the military. Quite naturally, all these factors lead to social apathy within society. The corruption is of a systemic nature, and society does not trust the authorities. Society sceptically notes that instead of real fight against corruption, the authorities have simply sacrificed yet another one of their disgraced representatives – whose inheritance is then immediately split between favoured oligarchs, in full view of the public.

9. Azerbaijan: Capacity for Change?

The Authorities

The authorities announce that they are in favour of the democratisation of society, but that one cannot over-facilitate or impose such processes, since the state may then find itself in the hands of ochlocracy or of crazy managers. They also love to speak of Azerbaijan's 'special path of development' towards democracy. And yet, they have again managed to create a parliament by relying on the old format: a parliament that is obedient and without any principles. Any outsider aspirations of gaining a seat in parliament are branded by the authorities as an attempt at gaining the supreme power and, in their eyes, are thus unjustifiable. Meanwhile, society itself is seen to be a somewhat underdeveloped, embryonic creature, incapable of making the right choice without hints from the 'top'.

The Opposition

An Imitation of Democracy
The opposition, for their part, argue that the authorities are only imitating democracy. Additionally, they argue that, in reality, the authorities are willing to preserve the existing corrupt bureaucratic regime, and that they are even resorting to the entire tool-kit of totalitarianism. The opposition wanted to have an honest fight for a seat in parliament, but this did not happen. It is for this reason that the rage of the revolutionary rhetoric on the eve of elections was indeed justified. It reflected not only the protest against the existing order, but also the protest against the subconscious feeling of being 'doomed'.

Attitudes within society
The opposition also believes that society is, to an equal degree, cautious about drastic changes and the maintenance of the current state of affairs. It does not favour politicians, and went into the shadow happily, surrendering the political arena to the politicians. But changes are inevitable, as is the choice of society. They are motivated not only by the well-known external re-

alities, but also by the internal situation in the country. The opposition is accused of being destructive, yet this destruction is provoked to a far greater degree by conflicts within the ruling elite, which are becoming ever more embittered. For example, the head of the capital's police force has publicly made serious accusations against the Minister of the Interior.[15]. In turn, the Minister of the Interior has spoken of assignments of the President of the country which were not to be discussed publicly anywhere in the world.[16] The Minister claimed that, in 1997, upon instruction from the president, he organised the prison escape of some members of Abuzar Abuzarov who were arrested in Azerbaijan. Seemingly, this was at the request of the mayor of the Dagestani city of Derbent (who justified this request by saying that the minister could help to organise the hypothetical protection of the 120,000 Azerbaijani population of this city). Furthermore, in the pre-election political confusion, the Minister of Education personally selected students for a master's programme abroad, although this function had already been delegated to another agency.

This destructiveness is further made clear if we take a look at the polarisation of the mass media prior to the elections: various journalists collected compromising data on the former Minister of Economic Development, and also against the head of customs. The complete merger of the political and economic elite in the country turned out to be a major problem for the state. As yet the process has remained manageable, but it is gradually moving beyond state control. The difficult yet best decision is for a transformation of the system from the top – but this is hardly possible without the procedures required in order to limit the power and guarantee the accountability of the authorities to society. In large measure this explains the embittered nature of the recent fight for the parliament, which stood out as one chance to create a healthy society.

However, just as in many of other oil-producing countries, the authorities are still relaxed and generous in promising a fantastic economic future. On the other hand, the opposition sometimes imposes the feeling of an upcoming catastrophe, a feeling not generally shared in society. People work hard for their living, and they follow the inflation and the enrichment of the ruling elite.

---

15 Turan agency, political news, 29 September 2005
16 ANS TV Channel, Interview with Minister of Interior Ramil Usubov, 24 July 2005.

And they hardly think that the main point is that Carthage should be destroyed immediately. The extreme economic assessment also confuses the people and in turn polarises society.

The Observations of Etibar Mamedov
We should note an interesting observation of one of the leaders of a moderate section of the opposition, who pointed out that power in Azerbaijan is concentrated in the hands of a small group of people who have money and power, but that this group is just as small as the opposition, which had lost the broad support of society. This is observation was made by Etibar Mamedov, leader of the Party of National Independence, once a central opposition activist, who lost much of his political baggage in recent years. It is possible that this statement was dictated by hurt feelings, since he is no longer accepted by the authorities or by the opposition. But at least in terms of the current political momentum there is one piece of truth in it: in the upcoming years, both parties will have to appeal to society and try to win its sympathies. The opportunities for the authorities seem to be wider in this case. However, the authorities, as the ruling entities, are also more vulnerable. In any case, this can provide a sort of a chance for society. The capacity for change will grow within the economy as well, although it is vital to distinguish clearly between illusion and reality.

Problems in Terms of Dynamics

Nevertheless, as noted above, the Azerbaijani economy may look fairly healthy. It is only when we start to assess it in terms of dynamics that we begin to notice how complicated the situation is. Firstly, it is becoming more and more difficult to address the emerging macroeconomic difficulties. They are multiplying, and they have to be addressed. For example, if the government does not facilitate structural economic reforms, and does not undertake a series of other serious measures, the exchange rate of the manat will keep rising all the way until 2011. Secondly, fully-fledged economic development can be continued only on the basis of serious export incentives, on the improved productivity in certain sectors, and on the establishment of a competitive economic environment. As of yet there has been no disaster, but it is possible in the future.

Currently only the sectors that are in the hands of the ruling economic elite are proving cost-efficient, primarily thanks to protectionism and monopolies. However, even their success is not a given, since, as a rule, the owners (usually an oligarch) do not want to resort to the services of managers, seeing them as simply an extra mouth to feed, and that, when property is separated from management, they are not an element of development. These owners portray a manager as some sort of thief who seeks to steal their property and become a millionaire. Many managers in the world do indeed become millionaires, but this is thanks to their talent, energy, and, not least, thanks to the perfectly legal ownership of the enterprise's capital. But the Azerbaijani oligarchs do not want to share. The problems, it appears, boil down to the fact that good managers need a transparent picture of the company. The general belief is that one does not want to give it to 'alien' managers, but to 'our own' managers – and they are a critically small group.

Let us look at these problems from another angle. A real strengthening of the national currency is always a reflection of the strengthening of the economy. But this has barely anything to do with Azerbaijan, where not a single reform has been completed, and the one-sided development of the sector of natural resources is apparent. The growing flow of oil dollars will keep stimulating demand, not supply. 'Gastarbeiter' money remittances from Azerbaijanis working in Russia, Ukraine and Turkey (barely recorded in the economy) also contribute to the same thing. Azerbaijan should have increased the supply in the economy; this relates to the sphere of small and medium-sized enterprises (SMEs). However, to put it kindly, SMEs in the country are extremely restrained. At the same time, the value of this economic group is unquestionable: it responds flexibly to changes in the economy and is capable of a providing a sensitive regulation of supply in the economy. SMEs secure half of the GDPs of many advanced economies. However, in Azerbaijan today this group is lost in trying to preserve themselves in the non-market environment.

These statements may come across as unfair. In the end, in 2005, a figure of 200 billion 'old' manat has been allocated for the purposes of developing this sector, and next year this figure will rise to 400 billion. However, the procedure for the distribution of credits from the national fund for the support of entrepreneurs (the group that has been allocated these privileged credits) remains closed, even in the circumstances of the seeming publicity, in terms of project assessment, and allocated funds. In the entrepreneurial environment, distrust towards banks (there was a common practice, known as 'hats', whereby bribes were made to bank officials for the purpose of getting loan allocations etc.) is now being replaced by distrust towards the Ministry of Economic Development. This distrust is further exacerbated by the fact that there is no data on the efficiency of the crediting of any SME, even though these loans have already been handed out for several years now.

Instead, we are informed that, as a result of this crediting, 25,000 jobs have been created – a fact which is impossible to check. It would be far more interesting to hear a story of an enterprise whose productivity doubled as a result of crediting, and of the purchase of modern equipment and good management. Unfortunately, the process of establishing a technological park, and industrial settlements, takes too long, even though these generally motivate the development of small and medium sized enterprises. To this we should add the fact that the emerged financial and industrial groups almost never resort to the services of SMEs, at a time when the government keeps reproaching major transnational companies for not involving local entrepreneurs in their work. However, in all developed countries, this type of business has, for a long time, been grouping around major enterprises, and this is the global development trend for SMEs. At the same time, the government never let a chance pass by to reproach major transnational companies for not involving local entrepreneurs in their work.

These topics have been emphasised because they relate to the process of the democratisation of relations in capital. It may appear naïve, but democratic relations in the environment of major capital (in the relations of the major capital and less successful SME colleagues) are an integral part of the process of democratisation of society.

Oil Strategy

The country's problems also include the persistent uncertainty over the strategy of how to use the resources of the Azerbaijani oil fund. True, there are some objective difficulties involved in this issue, but it is also apparent that the government is unwilling to lose control over these huge resources. This will happen as soon as the activities of the fund get straightened out and accountable to society. The objective of such funds is not usually limited to 'insuring' the future of the economy. It is also about giving a signal to domestic and foreign investors that the economy is quite solvent. It goes without saying that when the stabilisation fund is kept above a certain level, this significantly improves the investment attractiveness of the country. This amount will differ from country to country, and relates to the balance of payments of the country and to foreign debt. However, since this limit has not been set, its upper limit varies arbitrarily.

This in turn leads to constant macroeconomic disputes with regard to any of the stabilisation funds. For the Azerbaijani economy to work without recessions, money has to keep coming back into this fund, at a minimum level of the amount of what was taken out (oil also has this feature: it is irreplaceably taken out of the national wealth of the country) plus the inflation percentage. Yet everything seems to be happening in quite the contrary manner, with money being taken from the country's economy and kept in foreign banks. The objection to this is simple enough: in Azerbaijan, there are barely any non-oil industries to 'digest' these oil dollars. Although this objection is probably true, in practice this leads once again to the fact that the problems have to be addressed through the rational evaluation of the economy, the need for a clear assessment of the cost-efficiency of various sectors, and the permanent monitoring of productivity in such sectors, recording growth aspects.

Handling the Inflow of Foreign Currency

The expected inflow of foreign currency into Azerbaijan in *2006* is estimated to be USD 2 billion, of which USD 1.1 billion will be used within the country (to service foreign debt and to purchase conveyances and equipment that make it possible to prevent additional inflation). However, the Azerbaijani economy still has very few financial 'pumps' that would enable the excess money to be directed out of the economy. The oil fund alone is not enough for these purposes. For example, the relatively high level of inflation in Russia is explained by the fact that the country also lacks such 'pumps'; an accumulative pension system is just in the making in this country, and its stabilisation fund has not been institutionalised to any degree observable in the oil funds.[17] Here the appeals of the economic bloc to the government of Azerbaijan to liberalise the export of currency from the country are no accident. The head of the national bank has previously spoken about this on several occasions, and on New Year's Eve the Minister of Finance made a reminder about this very opportunity.[18]

Yet the expansion of Azerbaijani capital outside of the country would appear to be even more effective, although this should be accompanied by the monitoring of the employment situation in the country. One example is Kazakhstan, which has been decisively entering other countries with its capital; we might recall the participation of the Kazakh capital in various enterprises in Ukraine, Lithuania, and Georgia. In Georgia, Kazakhstan is ready to participate in the construction of high-voltage power lines, the construction of a tourist resort in Kobuleti, and in the purchases of Tbilgas shares. Kazakhstan's biggest bank, Turanalem, has started working in Azerbaijan, having become the channel for the expansion of the Kazakh capital abroad. The bank is ready to be involved in all types of activities in Azerbaijan, including financing enterprises, mortgaging and leasing.

As yet, Azerbaijan has no such plans. So far, the sole effective expansion of Azerbaijani capital abroad has been the purchase of an oil terminal in Jurjuleshti, Moldova, by the Azpetrol company. But it seems that this deal is also in jeopardy (although, in January, the President of Moldova made several optimistic statements about further development of this investment deal). However, this deal is probably jeopardised. It would be excellent if Azerbaijan could invest more effectively in Georgia, particularly in regions with an Azerbaijani population. Back in May 2005, Azerbaijan's Minister of Finance announced the possible participation of Azerbaijan in the core capital of the Georgian port in Batumi and Poti. Here we might recall the Ukrainian proposal for a joint venture in order to transport Caspian oil to Europe via the Odessa–Brody route. In other words, capital is growing in the country, and its

17 See article by Peter Svoik in the compendium *Kazakhstan and Russia*.
18 In an interview on ANS TV channel, 29 December.

external expansion would be a health promotion exercise for the economy, which has begun to have 'hot' money.

The development of fine-tuned mechanisms for funnelling oil dollars into the national economy continues to be a top item on the agenda. During the period of inflow of big money, every major economic activity of the state should be strictly evaluated against its possible consequences. The country has now established the State Investment Fund, and this in turn requires the establishment of a development bank and/or an investment bank. The investment fund itself may become a new catalyst for inflation unless public investments are scrupulously thought through and targeted towards a long-term effect – and also at blocking the overflow of this money to the consumer market, as this inevitably leads to inflation. Furthermore, the state should constantly be preoccupied with the nature and the speed of the return of this money back into economy. It can be difficult to calculate the effect of the development of infrastructural projects, for which this fund will primarily be working, on the economy. For example, road development will require a projection of the future transit expected on these roads. Unfortunately, such evaluations are very rare in Azerbaijan.

There are plenty of other fine nuances in the work of investment funds. It is important to assess not only the direction of investments, but also the formalisation of their use. Just as in the neighbouring countries, the funds of Azerbaijan's investment fund should be allocated to projects with a pre-set ceiling cost. These projects cannot, and should not, be either excessively cost-efficient or working at a loss. There will always be an investor for an extremely cost-efficient project, and the targeted public investments should be reasonably aimed at implementing these unprofitable but socially important projects. It is interesting to note, for example, that in Russia there is a provision whereby the profitability of projects receiving investments from the fund should be below the average profitability across the country. In terms of form, the state should pursue the establishment of public–private corporations in important sectors of the economy, with a future transfer of constructed objects into the private investor on a concession basis. This country should have strong and serious private companies, capable of participation in infrastructural projects.

Implementing the Reforms from Above: Associated Problems

Corruption

The opportunity for Azerbaijan to implement reforms from the top has not yet been exhausted, but it is rapidly diminishing. The corruption and monopolisation of all spheres of economy become a serious obstacle to even the seemingly most rational steps of the government. In particular, the regional development programme (which is, in essence, positive) quickly turns into a 'corruption-feeder'. Corruption is most dangerous in places where it blocks the development of a competitive business environment. Not surprisingly, the establishment of an export promotion fund has constantly faced problems. Lobbyists are themselves frequently invisible, yet their activities are quite visible, and the permanent source of corruption – mutual non-payments in the main economic sectors – persists.

For a long time, corruption found justification in the difficulties of the transition period. Representatives of the authorities love to repeat this simple thesis: corruption is everywhere. However, unless it faces resistance, the corruption monster tends to spread and lead a life of its own. Here we should recall that, by the mid-1990s, the idea of legalising shadow capital caused an outburst of rage within society. Today, society has put up with this proposal and even finds positive aspects in it, yet it seems that this is something that the ruling power itself does not oppose. If this capital becomes legalised, the ruling power could lose its final levers of influence on the management centres at the top bureaucratic level. Moreover, these centres are starting to behave quite independently.

For all these reasons, the authorities prefer to preserve the corruption pyramid in the shape that it is in today. Thus the chances of at least a partial dismantlement of this pyramid are diminishing, for example, in such socially important spheres as education and healthcare. After recent events involving the replacement of the top leadership in the Ministry of Health, serious reforms are expected to start only after revisions are made to the system of medical education, the strict attestation of doctors and the introduction of principles of health insurance. In the judiciary, the corruption spree has only worsened. The year of the official fight against corruption failed to bring any tangible results – except for the arrests of several heads of district military commissariats in Baku, but this is only at the medium level of the corruption pyramid. Furthermore, those in power do not want to record the arrests of corrupt major bureaucrats as an anti-corruption measure, since that would inevitably disclose the fairly serious corruption mechanisms still at work in the country.

Democracy is the Sole Alternative

Further economic development becomes problematic even without the issue of the democratisation of the public structure of the country. One cannot live under an illusion for too long, for instance, regarding to the 'corruption lubricant'. And one cannot build an open market economy under conditions whereby the judiciary and the legislative branches are subordinate to the executive, to state-oligarchic capitalism, and to the growing outrageousness of monopolies. In this sense, there are no alternatives to democracy in Azerbaijan – whether it begins from the top, with the authorities, or with the people, fighting from the bottom.

Unfortunately, the resolve of the authorities to effectively fight corruption raises great doubts. References to the fact that some countries have managed to develop economically without democracy are ill-founded: this happens only where there is a sustainable tradition of private property (as in Chile), whereas Azerbaijan is a country that is, in all respects, in transition from totalitarianism to a new authoritarianism – in turn building the new 'rationale' of the principles relating to democracy and market relations.

For these reasons, it is becoming harder and harder to reanimate the lost pace of economic reforms which have fallen hostage to politics. In many areas of reform, Azerbaijan lags far behind Russia and Kazakhstan, and sometimes this backwardness appears impossible to overcome. Thus, according to the evaluations of economist G. Ibadogly,[19] given that we achieve the annual budgetary growth of 25%, planned from 2006, the growth of the average wage in 2006 will be equal to that of Russia in 2005. And when, in 2009, the country achieves a GDP per capita of USD 2000, this will be equal to the Ka-

---

19   In the newspaper *Musavat* 26.12.05

zakh indicator of 2001. Add to this the peculiarity of the corruption mechanisms, which turn the problems relating to the quality of goods and services
into a secondary issue. It appears necessary to develop the kind of innovations that will require privileges for the import of new technologies into the
country. Although the President did declare that the country has its own capacity for implementing a series of projects, the advantage of direct foreign
investments is self-evident: new investments are usually accompanied by
capital, as well as by new technologies and the culture of management.

Finally, no matter how harsh the games of the West may seem, Azerbaijanis should get used to the thought that, unless their country involves itself in
global games, it will not advance at the expense of oil dollars alone. Impera-
tive here is accession to the World Trade Organisation, with consequent market liberalisation.

From a sober perspective, the authorities would certainly develop long-term
development trends for the country, trends that would not only reflect the level
of the country's revenues from oil and the transit of oil, but also from the perspective of directions for growth. As yet there is not a single survey devoted
to even a rough calculation of the national wealth of the country. Furthermore,
nobody monitors the Gross Domestic Product, although only GDP can provide an unambiguous picture of economic development. In reality, little is
known about the productivity of various sectors, and about the ultimate demand and supply across the economy. But we can be quite hopeful about the
fact that the work on developing a employment strategy for 2006–2015 has
finally been completed, and may hope that it will reflect the evaluations of effective employment in the country. Azerbaijan has launched a system of national accounts which quite accurately informs us of the painful points in the
economy. Immediately after the first accounts were issued in 2002, the State
Statistic Committee made issues for 2003–2004. Unfortunately, there are few
users of this serious product among economists, whether state or non-
governmental. Finally, the government has shown almost no interest in introducing a population register, even though active migration processes make
this field extremely important. Prior to the parliamentary elections, a complete
register of voters was never created (such a register could easily have been
updated between the elections), even though this is what the European structures insistently recommended. The introduction of the accumulative pension

fund system will definitely force a return to the idea of a register of voters, although under Azerbaijani conditions this will involve the well-known dangers for the citizens of the country with regard to 'having control' over them. Such worries are already visible in Russia. Azerbaijan is a small country, so a meticulous statistical review of the economy could become a significant element for the energetic and foolproof development of the economy.

10. Conclusions

The moment of truth has come for Azerbaijan: one must learn to distinguish between politics and the economy. As long the complete system of symbiosis continues to rule supreme, it does not appear possible for the country to make a normal transition towards a market economy. Instead, the market economy will remain imitative in nature, just as the case is with the Azerbaijani democracy.

The post-election situation proved to be a crisis of sorts. Hopes for the West, as well as a revolution from the top and from the bottom, have been exhausted. The sole hope that remains lies with the changing generations, without which, it seems, nothing will happen. There is the possibility of an external push – as with a war between the USA and Iran, or the continuation of the war with Armenia – but the state, unprepared for these events, will find itself in an even worse situation, defined by the temporary rule of 'patriotic' forces. Some hopes were pinned on the January session of PACE, as this was supposed to discuss and decide on the parliamentary elections in Azerbaijan. In the case of sanctions of this organisation, and the facilitated movement of Azerbaijan in the direction of Russia, Azerbaijan would have a chance for a quick growth of political activity in the country. However, although the issue of depriving the Azerbaijani delegation of its voting power (until the summer PACE session) was discussed three times in the commissions of the parliament, the mandate of the Azerbaijani delegation was eventually approved, although with significant reservations and recommendations.

The most dangerous thing about the authoritarian rule of the country is that it sees society as a destructive force. The authoritarian power dwells on itself, and is less partial to any kinds of partnership with society. The authorities are equally worried by the development of the municipalities and the growth of NGOs in the country. This is even more surprising since the chairpersons of the municipal associations and enterprises are mostly members of the ruling party 'Eni Azerbaijan?' Furthermore, at least half of the NGOs are quite successfully controlled by the authorities themselves.

It is enough to note the statement of a member of parliament (a brother of the previous President and an uncle of the present one) to evaluate the general situation in the country: 'NGOs create disorders and confusion around the globe. They is created to rob the wealth of their countries. Everyone who believes himself a patriot should treat NGOs as enemies, and one should fight them.' (*Zerkalo*, 16.06.05)

However, there are also reasons for optimism. The Azerbaijani democratic opposition still exists, and it continues its activities despite all attempts of the authorities to provoke it into a forceful standoff and finally destroy it. Furthermore, society is slowly getting richer, and will inevitably create the momentum for change. As noted by Russian political expert Boris Kagarlitsky 'A hungry person does not have the strength or the energy for a riot. Revolutions happen when a satisfied person is left hungry for one day'. Finally, despite everything, within the authorities themselves, the effect caused by the fact that the major economic groups are becoming autonomous from the current authorities, will grow. Initial attempts have not succeeded, but this does not mean that no further attempts will follow. Azerbaijani capital will definitely look for a basis in society.

In the end, nobody has ever refuted the laws of economics. As soon as the economic system starts to slow down and serious economic crises emerge, the 'Siamese' political and economic parts of the authorities will find themselves in a tough standoff.

Dr. Andreas Umland (Ed.)

SOVIET AND POST-SOVIET
POLITICS AND SOCIETY

ISSN 1614-3515

This book series makes available, to the academic community and general public, affordable English-, German- and Russian-language scholarly studies of various *empirical* aspects of the recent history and current affairs of the former Soviet bloc. The series features narrowly focused research on a variety of phenomena in Central and Eastern Europe as well as Central Asia and the Caucasus. It highlights, in particular, so far understudied aspects of late Tsarist, Soviet, and post-Soviet political, social, economic and cultural history from 1905 until today. Topics covered within this focus are, among others, political extremism, the history of ideas, religious affairs, higher education, and human rights protection. In addition, the series covers selected aspects of post-Soviet transitions such as economic crisis, civil society formation, and constitutional reform.

SOVIET AND POST-SOVIET POLITICS AND SOCIETY

Edited by Dr. Andreas Umland

ISSN 1614-3515

38   *Josette Baer (Ed.)*
      Preparing Liberty in Central Europe
      Political Texts from the Spring of Nations 1848 to the Spring of Prague 1968
      With a foreword by Zdeněk V. David
      ISBN 3-89821-546-6

39   *Михаил Лукьянов*
      Российский консерватизм и реформа, 1907-1914
      С предисловием Марка Д. Стейнберга
      ISBN 3-89821-503-2

40   *Nicola Melloni*
      Market Without Economy
      The 1998 Russian Financial Crisis
      With a foreword by Eiji Furukawa
      ISBN 3-89821-407-9

41   *Dmitrij Chmelnizki*
      Die Architektur Stalins
      Bd. 1: Studien zu Ideologie und Stil
      Bd. 2: Bilddokumentation
      Mit einem Vorwort von Bruno Flierl
      ISBN 3-89821-515-6

42   *Katja Yafimava*
      Post-Soviet Russian-Belarussian Relationships
      The Role of Gas Transit Pipelines
      With a foreword by Jonathan P. Stern
      ISBN 3-89821-655-1

43   *Boris Chavkin*
      Verflechtungen der deutschen und russischen Zeitgeschichte
      Aufsätze und Archivfunde zu den Beziehungen Deutschlands und der Sowjetunion von 1917 bis 1991
      Ediert von Markus Edlinger sowie mit einem Vorwort versehen von Leonid Luks
      ISBN 3-89821-756-6

44   *Anastasija Grynenko in Zusammenarbeit mit Claudia Dathe*
      Die Terminologie des Gerichtswesens der Ukraine und Deutschlands im Vergleich
      Eine übersetzungswissenschaftliche Analyse juristischer Fachbegriffe im Deutschen, Ukrainischen und
      Russischen
      Mit einem Vorwort von Ulrich Hartmann
      ISBN 3-89821-691-8

45   *Anton Burkov*
      The Impact of the European Convention on Human Rights on Russian Law
      Legislation and Application in 1996-2006
      With a foreword by Françoise Hampson
      ISBN 978-3-89821-639-5

46   *Stina Torjesen, Indra Overland (Eds.)*
      International Election Observers in Post-Soviet Azerbaijan
      Geopolitical Pawns or Agents of Change?
      ISBN 978-3-89821-743-9

FORTHCOMING (MANUSCRIPT WORKING TITLES)

Stephanie Solowyda
Biography of Semen Frank
ISBN 3-89821-457-5

Margaret Dikovitskaya
Arguing with the Photographs
Russian Imperial Colonial Attitudes in Visual Culture
ISBN 3-89821-462-1

Stefan Ihrig
Welche Nation in welcher Geschichte?
Eigen- und Fremdbilder der nationalen Diskurse in der Historiographie und den Geschichtsbüchern in der Republik Moldova, 1991-2003
ISBN 3-89821-466-4

Sergei M. Plekhanov
Russian Nationalism in the Age of Globalization
ISBN 3-89821-484-2

Robert Pyrah
Cultural Memory and Identity
Literature, Criticism and the Theatre in Lviv - Lwow - Lemberg, 1918-1939 and in post-Soviet Ukraine
ISBN 3-89821-505-9

Andrei Rogatchevski
The National-Bolshevik Party
ISBN 3-89821-532-6

Zenon Victor Wasyliw
Soviet Culture in the Ukrainian Village
The Transformation of Everyday Life and Values, 1921-1928
ISBN 3-89821-536-9

Nele Sass
Das gegenkulturelle Milieu im postsowjetischen Russland
ISBN 3-89821-543-1

Julie Elkner
Maternalism versus Militarism
The Russian Soldiers' Mothers Committee
ISBN 3-89821-575-X

Maryna Romanets
Displaced Subjects, Anamorphosic Texts, Reconfigured Visions
Improvised Traditions in Contemporary Ukrainian and Irish Literature
ISBN 3-89821-576-8

Alexandra Kamarowsky
Russia's Post-crisis Growth
ISBN 3-89821-580-6

Martin Friessnegg
Das Problem der Medienfreiheit in Russland seit dem Ende der Sowjetunion
ISBN 3-89821-588-1

Nikolaj Nikiforowitsch Borobow
Führende Persönlichkeiten in Russland vom 12. bis 20 Jhd.: Ein Lexikon
Aus dem Russischen übersetzt und herausgegeben von Eberhard Schneider
ISBN 3-89821-638-1

Martin Malek, Anna Schor-Tschudnowskaja
Tschetschenien und die Gleichgültigkeit Europas
Russlands Kriege und die Agonie der Idee der Menschenrechte
ISBN 3-89821-676-4

Christopher Ford
Borotbism A Chapter in the History of the Ukrainian Revolution
ISBN 3-89821-697-7

Taras Kuzio, Paul D'Anieri (Hrsg.)
Aspects of the Orange Revolution I: Regime Politics and Democratization in Ukraine
ISBN 3-89821-698-5

Bohdan Harasymiw, Oleh S. Ilnytzkyj (Hrsg.)
Aspects of the Orange Revolution II: Analyses of the 2004 Ukrainian Presidential Elections
ISBN 3-89821-699-3

Togzhan Kassenova
Cooperative Security in the Post-Cold War International System
The Cooperative Threat Reduction Process
ISBN 3-89821-707-8

Andreas Langenohl
Political Culture and Criticism of Society
Intellectual Articulations in Post-Soviet Russia
ISBN 3-89821-709-4

Marlies Bilz
Tatarstan in der Transformation, 1988-1994
ISBN 3-89821-722-1

Thomas Borén
Meeting Places in Transformation
ISBN 3-89821-739-6

Lars Löckner
Sowjetrussland in der Beurteilung der Emigrantenzeitung 'Rul', 1920-1924
ISBN 3-89821-741-8

Ekaterina Taratuta
The Red Line of Construction
Semantics and Mythology of a Siberian Heliopolis
ISBN 3-89821-742-6

Bernd Kappenberg
Zeichen setzen für Europa
Der Gebrauch europäischer lateinischer Sonderzeichen in der deutschen Öffentlichkeit
ISBN 3-89821-749-3

Series Subscription

Please enter my subscription to the series *Soviet and Post-Soviet Politics and Society*, ISSN 1614-3515, as follows:

❐ complete series   OR   ❐ English-language titles
                                        ❐ German-language titles
                                        ❐ Russian-language titles

starting with
❐ volume # 1
❐ volume # ___
    ❐ please also include the following volumes: #___, ___, ___, ___, ___, ___, ___
❐ the next volume being published
    ❐ please also include the following volumes: #___, ___, ___, ___, ___, ___, ___

❐ 1 copy per volume   OR   ❐ ___ copies per volume

Subscription within Germany:

You will receive every volume at 1st publication at the regular bookseller's price – incl. s & h and VAT.
Payment:
❐ Please bill me for every volume.
❐ Lastschriftverfahren: Ich/wir ermächtige(n) Sie hiermit widerruflich, den Rechnungsbetrag je Band von meinem/unserem folgendem Konto einzuziehen.

Kontoinhaber: _____ Kreditinstitut: _____
Kontonummer: _____ Bankleitzahl: _____

International Subscription:

Payment (incl. s & h and VAT) in advance for
❐ 10 volumes/copies (€ 319.80)   ❐ 20 volumes/copies (€ 599.80)
❐ 40 volumes/copies (€ 1,099.80)
Please send my books to:

NAME_____ DEPARTMENT_____
ADDRESS _____
POST/ZIP CODE_____ COUNTRY _____
TELEPHONE _____ EMAIL_____

date/signature_____

A hint for librarians in the former Soviet Union: Your academic library might be eligible to receive free-of-cost scholarly literature from Germany via the German Research Foundation. For Russian-language information on this program, see
    http://www.dfg.de/forschungsfoerderung/formulare/download/12_54.pdf.

Please fax to: **0511 / 262 2201 (+49 511 262 2201)**
or mail to: *ibidem*-Verlag, Julius-Leber-Weg 11, D-30457 Hannover, Germany
or send an e-mail: ibidem@ibidem-verlag.de

ibidem-Verlag

Melchiorstr. 15

D-70439 Stuttgart

info@ibidem-verlag.de

www.ibidem-verlag.de
www.edition-noema.de
www.autorenbetreuung.de

www.ingramcontent.com/pod-product-compliance
Lightning Source LLC
Chambersburg PA
CBHW062022270326

41929CB00014B/2281